After the Due Order

"For because ye [did it] not at the first, the LORD
our God made a breach upon us, for that we sought
him not after the due order." I Chronicles 15:13

After the Due Order

"For because ye [did it] not at the first, the LORD our God made a breach upon us, for that we sought him not after the due order." I Chronicles 15:13

by
Larry Gordon

THE NAME
MINISTRIES
Sergeant Bluff, Iowa

After the Due Order
ISBN 0-9627779-0-0
Copyright © 1990 by **The Name Ministries**
R.R. #1, Box 28
Sergeant Bluff, IA 51054

Published by **The Name Ministries**
R.R. #1, Box 28
Sergeant Bluff, IA 51054

Contents

Dedication

In memory of Dr. Russ Martin, my pastor of 21 years at First Christian Church in Miami, Oklahoma. He first caused my heart to stir and understand that the church must be guided by the pastor.

Acknowledgements

My heartfelt thanks to my wonderful wife and best friend Eileen and to Kraig Wall my associate. Both have given much time and vigilance into the editing of this work!

Acknowledgments

Foreword

The book you have in your hand is not a book of new revelation. It is a book that comes into the flow of our day of restoration. It brings forth God's due order in the Church. After 2,000 years of man's good ideas, we must now turn away from the hopeless mess they have made with the Church and start afresh with God's plan.

Who could better write this book than the pastor of a local church? Larry Gordon has meticulously searched the Scripture and brought forth the plan of God. For those champions of democracy, this book may seem to be heresy, but please remember that when you deal with God's ways, they will not be our ways (Isaiah 55:8). A theocratic government is not new, so as you read, do not be totally guided by your first impressions. All of us are products of tradition and traditional teaching which tends to make the Word of God of no effect.

I heartily recommend this book to all the Church as a breath of fresh air in the midst of human ideas.

John Avanzini

Foreword

It was my pleasure to read the manuscript for Pastor Larry Gordon's "After the Due Order". These pastoral thoughts and concepts were birthed in his heart over the last few years as a result of the vibrant and dynamic ministry the Lord has given him. Cornerstone Faith Center in Sioux City, Iowa has an external attraction because of its awesome worship and anointed Biblical teaching and preaching. The church also has an internal cohesion and staff camaraderie due to Pastor Gordon's wise leadership.

This book is compiled from a series of seven Sunday sermons delivered to the congregation. While some of the statements may seem repetitious to you, do remember that in a series of this nature it is common to reiterate certain key points for the sake of impact. Pastor Gordon has wisely reminded his Sunday audience of key points given in his previous messages. Reading these chapters as sermons made the material that much more lucid to me.

The present day pastor does not have it easy. There is an anti-authority spirit in our society. Rebellion is openly encouraged by our media. By refusing to submit to a local church, its policies, its disciplines, and its authority, a maverick breed of independents has surfaced. These people want to have a religious faith with all the benefits minus commitment. Pastors are put in a bad light by these lone ranger believers. This book, "After the Due Order", shows from a Biblical perspective the vital need for a congregation to have a caring pastor.

Another stress area all pastors face is the renewed emphasis on the five-fold ministries. Apostles and prophets are definitely in the spiritual emphasis of many groups with a new and concentrated focus on five-fold ministries. Many pastors have been reduced to an unnecessary appendage or a reduced level of importance. Pastor Larry's book wisely and clearly shows the pastor as being the vital link. The local church makes it possible for apostles and prophets to function. The local church also gives impetus to evangelists and teachers.

I'm sure your appreciation for all local church pastors will be reconfirmed as you read this book.

Dick Mills

Author's Notes

The following chapters are seven messages from the Spirit of God that were delivered to me in a most miraculous and anointed fashion during a time that they were desperately needed in the life of my congregation. The results were dramatic. For the most part the people of God could breathe a sigh of relief over a question that has plagued the churches for years.

As a young man I was nurtured and taught well the fantastic tenets of liberty and democracy. While those tenets are God-given and are the most fruitful and life-giving principles for national and state governments, we encounter extreme difficulties when we begin to use those ideas in the church.

The pages that follow are not designed to be a great literary work that will awe the reader with dramatic style and flowing prose. These chapters are sermons that I delivered to the flock of God. The content is of significance. The complete scope of this message will unfold much more clearly as the chapters progress. It is my hope that you will follow with me through to the end to see the full picture of what I feel the Spirit desires to bring forth through my admittedly human efforts. In order to stress important points to the minds of the reader, certain subjects have been covered on a number of occasions in this writing; but the message within will bring life and understanding to those who are ready and hungry to receive instruction from the Holy Spirit.

Every question and aspect of the "Due Order" of God could not be covered in one writing; and yet I know the great liberty and security these messages brought to Cornerstone Faith Center.

It is my fervent desire that anyone who may read these pages will be blessed of God with a better understanding of how to flow in God's great plan for His church in these glorious last days.

In His Strong Name,
Pastor Larry Gordon

The Theocracy of God

CHAPTER

We are living in the end of time; and in the end of time God said that He was coming for a bride without spot, wrinkle or blemish. Today He is preparing the bride to be what He always intended it to be. It seems that every time God has a good idea and turns it over to man, the idea gets perverted.

In every living program of earth, particularly in the midst of rapid growth, there are introduced those administrative opportunities, cleverly disguised as problems to overcome, obstacles to hurdle. So it was in the sixth chapter of Acts in which we find the baby church, the infant church, facing its first dilemma concerning the Hellenist widows.

When we read the sixth chapter of Acts, we are not reading there a reference from which to draw information pertaining to establishing church government; rather we find there a description of the body of Christ as it was just being birthed from the womb of God in its evolutionary process to become what God desires it to be. Let's read it together:

> "And in those days, when the number of the disciples was multiplied, there arose a murmuring of the Grecians against the Hebrews, because their widows were neglected in the daily ministration. Then the twelve called the multitude of the disciples unto them, and said, It is not reason that we should leave the word of God, and serve tables. Wherefore, brethren, look ye out among you seven men of honest report, full of the Holy Ghost and wisdom, whom we may appoint over this business. But we will give ourselves continually to prayer, and to the ministry of the word. And the saying pleased the whole multitude: and they chose Stephen, a man full of faith and of the Holy Ghost, and Philip, and Prochorus, and Nicanor, and Timon, and Parmenas, and Nicolas a proselyte of Antioch: Whom they set before the Apostles: and when they had prayed, they laid their hands on them."   Acts 6:1-6

This is the record of the first growth problem of the baby church. It was an administrative problem: thank God for a church administrator.

Therefore, into the picture steps the Holy Spirit, the Administrator of God's worldwide church. He is a problem solver: He knows how to solve every problem that comes along. His answer to the problem was both practical and ingenious. As always, because He is God, it was the ultimate and most fruitful solution to the problem at hand.

Somehow, however, as is common to the characteristics of the human species, through the years this story, which is a very simple and beautiful story, has been misunderstood and misconstrued, until this fantastic narrative of God's wisdom has been twisted into one of the most bizarre and tragic mistakes of interpretation ever to occur. The error is found in much of the church worldwide. From this wonderful story of God's intervention into the affairs of man to save the day, men have gleaned a false doctrine. This doctrine strikes at the very center of what the church is all about. It strikes and threatens a death blow to her productivity and fruitfulness. Indeed because of this false presumption, multitudes of saints have been sidetracked and have rendered their churches impotent. They have found themselves without the Spirit's greatest might against the enemy. It was indeed the enemy himself who instigated this great misconception in the first place. What is this great hindrance that has time and again become the Waterloo of many potentially great moves of God? Here it is! Are you ready? It sounds very innocent and subtle. One of the worst doctrines ever introduced to the church world is this: THE CHURCH IS A DEMOCRACY.

The church is not a democracy. Democracy means "man-ruled". The church of the living God is a Theocracy. Theocracy means "God-ruled". God desires to rule His church!

You may say, "Democracy is what our beloved land is all about. It's the greatest form of civil government on earth. Under its tenets men have greater liberty and freedom than any other type of government on earth."

Dear friend, to that, I as a patriot and a lover of this great nation say a hearty "Amen!" Our land truly is America the beautiful! There is no other land on earth like our nation. I have been to other lands and then come flying home over New York Harbor and seeing that grand old lady standing there to welcome me home fought back tears; because there is no place like America. It is the greatest land on this planet. I wholeheartedly support and embrace our democracy and civil government.

In the church of the living God, however, it can never be so. The church is not man's possession. Men have made the mistake of thinking it was. Because men give offerings to the church, some have considered the church to be their own organization, much as one might buy membership in a social club. This misconception has fostered the idea that church membership should entitle one to a voice or vote in how things should be run; however, this is false. The church is God's! Some folks have the idea that the church is some type of business in which we are investing, and we have become part owners. Wrong! We give our tithe to the Lord, because " . . . all the tithe . . . is the Lord's: it is holy unto the Lord." (Lev. 27:30) Tithing and giving gives no man ownership in the church of the Living God. We are not share holders in God's church by virtue of the money we have given. We must understand that truth. In fact every last time the rulership of the church has passed out of the hands of God and into the hands of men, chaos and tragedy have been the result. We are not saying that democracy in all forms and situations is taboo in the church. There may be times when some decisions are made by voting: for instance, the Sunday school superintendent may ask his or her workers to decide something in that fashion. A pastor may want a vote taken on certain occasions when his purpose is to please the most people, but never when it might jeopardize God's plan. The pastor is responsible before God to lead the church as only God directs. For example, God may speak to a certain pastor to build a church. That pastor would be obligated to follow God's plan and build the church: there would not be any room to vote on the vision God places in His leader. However, the entire congregation may be polled to choose a carpet color for that same building. Never should the will of the people be allowed to override God's directives! When the overall government of the church is one of democratically voting on the business of the church, God's power will depart. When God's power departs, men are left alone. Men are left behind, unwittingly involved in playing a game of religious charades, acting out empty roles of nothingness, and calling it the church.

The church was never, never intended to be a democracy in any form. This does not elevate the pastor as a man, but it puts the five fold "ministry gifts" in proper perspective. In particular, in the church, it positions the pastor (ministry gift) as the earthly head of the church where God Almighty has placed him. We must separate the man from the function. A true pastor will never allow God's placement to result in pride: as a pastor I realize daily that I am nothing and the Lord in me is everything. Humanly speaking, ministry gifts are simply men as other men; however, they are elevated by God as the leaders of the local church. Pastors must build the church following the dictates of the Lord of the church as opposed to the dictates of the people.

We are living in the end of the earth. It is time for God's people to wake up, grow up, and realize that things are not necessarily the way we think they are, but as the scripture says they are.

It is my desire in this writing to show to the heart that is open to revelation and enlightenment, that the church is not and never was intended to be a democracy. To coin a phrase from our Lord, "He that hath an ear, let him hear what the Spirit saith unto the churches . . . ." (Rev. 2:7)

Daniel wrote, " . . . seal the book, to the time of the end: many shall run to and fro, and knowledge shall be increased." (Dan. 12:4) God is going to establish the revelation of His government to the churches who will listen. In the beginning of this writing, God began to awaken me on several mornings at 3:00 a.m. The Spirit urged me to get out of bed, take a tablet and pencil and write down the things that He would say to me. I was totally unaware of the subject matter until He began to reveal it to me as I wrote. This is a supernatural revelation from a supernatural God, Who desires to transform us into a supernatural church full of glory and power!

Having been educated within a conservative, evangelical, non-charismatic movement, I was taught, as were so many, that when we read Acts 6:1-6 we are reading God's proof text for democracy in the church. At the time of my former education it did not occur to me, nor to this day has it occurred to those who taught me, that the idea of "God's Democracy" is both antithetical and absurd, for by definition it would be "God's Man-Ruled Church".

The church was never intended to be a democracy. God must rule the church! He will not share His throne with any person who does not happen to be a member of the Trinity, the triune Godhead. Either God sits upon the throne in headship or man does. Should the latter be true and the church be run by the majority vote of man, we are all in desperate trouble.

Do you remember the church in the wilderness? Acts 7:38 says of Moses, the pastor of that church, "This is he that was in the church in the wilderness . . . ." Also, Numbers 20:4 says, "And why have you brought up the congregation of the Lord into this wilderness . . . ?" In the Old Testament Church with Pastor Moses and the assistant pastors Joshua, Caleb, Aaron and many others, there were three to six million people. Talk about administrative problems: they had them! Do you remember the awful price paid by that church and the horrible end that came by virtue of the first majority takeover? Why did it happen? They succumbed to man's rule in the place of God's rule. They placed themselves in direct opposition to the rule of God.

God had sent the twelve spies to go in and spy out the land in preparation to go in and take the promise of God. The thirteenth chapter of Numbers tells us that after they had spied out the land as God had commanded, ten of the twelve spies rebelled in fear. They brought back a fearful report which God referred to as an "evil report". They instilled that fear and doubt in the hearts of all of God's people. God dealt with that evil report, and He will deal with an evil report today that instills fear and anarchy in the flock of God. Moses dealt with it then: any good pastor will do so today. Here is the story:

> "And Caleb stilled the people, before Moses, and said, Let us go up at once, and possess it; for we are well able to overcome it. But the men that went up with him said, We be not able to go up against the people; for they are stronger than we. And they brought up an evil report of the land which they had searched out unto the children of Israel, saying, The land, through which we have gone to search it, is a land that eateth up the inhabitants thereof; and all the people that we saw in it are men of great stature. And there we saw the giants, the sons of Anak, which come of the giants: and we were in our own sight as grass-

hoppers, and so we were in their sight. And all the congregation lifted up their voice, and cried; and the people wept that night. And all the children of Israel murmured against Moses and against Aaron: and the whole congregation said unto them, Would God that we had died in the land of Egypt! or would God that we had died in this wilderness!" Numbers 13:30-14:2

These foolish Hebrews had in that moment cursed themselves by the majority vote to rebel against God; for when they rebelled against Moses, they rebelled against God. It would have been far better for them to have faced the giants in the land; for the anger of giants is dwarfed to impotence when compared to the anger they had brought upon themselves. The Hebrew writer expressed it so well in Hebrews 10:31, "It is a fearful thing to fall into the hands of the living God." Numbers 14:11 says, "And the Lord said unto Moses, How long will this people provoke me? . . . "

Now it was Moses they were proposing to stone; yet God said, "How long will this people provoke Me? and how long will it be ere they believe me, for all the signs which I have shewed among them?"

I believe there is a message there for you and for me. How many congregations have started with a handful of people and in just a miraculous few years have grown to hundreds of souls? The hand of God has been seen over and over again. Some of God's people, however, can find no good thing of which to speak. Complaining, murmuring and griping are the order of the day. Dear reader, we are living in a day in the end of the earth when to live a life of murmuring is to live dangerously. Verses 26-28 say:

"And the Lord spake unto Moses and unto Aaron, saying, How long shall I bear with this evil congregation, which murmur against me? I have heard the murmuring of the children of Israel, which they murmur against me. Say unto them, as truly as I live, saith the Lord, as ye have spoken in mine ears so will I do to you . . . ."

Be very careful what you say you wish God would do; for the Hebrews said they wished to God they had died in the wilderness; and that is exactly what happened. God graciously granted their stiff-necked and rebellious wish; and thus ends the story of the first democratic vote in the church in the wilderness. The children of Israel voted to overrule God and Pastor Moses, and they all perished in the wilderness. Their children were forced to wander for forty years around Mount Sinai. For forty years they knew no peace. They battled enemies on every hand because of the rebellion of their parents. Tragedy has been the outcome every time democratic methods have been introduced into a theocratic organism. As water is to gasoline, so democracy is to the church. The energy of God is diluted in any church that has men voting on God's business. God never intended it to be so! God is a God of order . . . His order, not man's order. He has marvelously ordered things to be most efficient, most productive and most life giving to the church, which is the object of His love.

God always has the perfect way. Proverbs 16:25 says, "There is a way that seemeth right unto a man, but the end thereof are the ways of death." Every church whose method of leadership is the majority vote of a board of men is in danger of never hearing from God. God will not operate as men think He should; neither will He wait for approval by majority vote regarding His plans for His church.

Certainly God does speak to boards of men who are seeking Him for direction; however His purpose is always to confirm what He has already spoken to the one He has chosen to lead, the pastor. The safety found in a multitude of counselors for a pastor is given to help him implement the vision God has placed within Him for the flock. Those with leadership qualities who are chosen by the pastor are to offer wisdom and confirmation to him; but they must never seek to override the authority God placed in him.

Jesus the Good Shepherd will always speak to His "under-shepherd", the pastor, about the leading of the flock. When it happens that one of the "sheep" believes God has spoken something to him which is contrary to the pastor's direction, it becomes the job of that "sheep" to pray and trust the leadership of the one God has called to lead. While it is true that all pastors are human and therefore subject to error, still they are "gifts" from God to direct His flock.

God does not want the minds of men involved with church government. He desires for us to be blessed above all men; and in this last day, just prior to the coming of the Lord, He is planting His government firmly into the minds and hearts of His people.

This is not meant to imply that God is giving His pastors a license to be dictators. A wise pastor will gather around himself men of wisdom to give him input in the decisions that he must make. Very few pastors are capable of handling in solo fashion the affairs of a rapidly prospering church. As each pastor is skilled in different areas, he will gather to himself those whose skills complement and augment his own. As a pastor, I am grateful for the fine group of men who give me input and expertise. But know this: God is reestablishing the theocracy now in the end of the earth.

On April 6, 1987, David Minor spoke a word from the Lord which was published in a paper through the "Endtime HandMaidens". He spoke of the two winds that were blowing. The first wind was to shake everything that can be shaken, and there has indeed been "a whole lot of shakin' goin' on". The church has done some reeling for all the world to see through the exposures of the late 1980's; but consider with me now the rest of the prophecy:

> "Be not dismayed for after this my wind will blow again. Have you not read how my breath blew on the valley of dry bones? So it shall breathe on you. This wind will come in equal force as the first wind. This wind, too, will have a name. It shall be called, THE KINGDOM OF GOD. IT SHALL BRING MY [*church*] GOVERNMENT AND ORDER . . . Along with that it shall bring my power. The supernatural shall come in that wind. The world will laugh at you for the devastation that comes in the first wind . . . "
> [Certainly we know that the world has laughed at the church in 1987 and 1988 with the downfall of some of the largest ministries in this world. In the local churches there have been some who have been shaken and have left.] " . . . but they will laugh no more. For

this wind will come with equal force and power that will produce the miraculous among my people. And the fear of God shall fall upon the nation." *(brackets added)*

Now, what is that revelation that is going to precipitate the power of God such as the world has never seen? We are not referring to local, state or federal authority, but His Church Government! His Order! There are two basic things that the worldwide church has not thoroughly understood; first, the theocracy, God's form of church government, and secondly, the finances of the church. Because the church has a problem understanding the government of God, it has stumbled at the subject of church finances; but when theocracy is understood, God's finances will be understood. The fears regarding those finances will also dissipate. When the government of God is understood, men will no longer cry, "What about accountability? To whom is our leader accountable?"

Let me tell you to whom any pastor is most assuredly accountable: he is accountable to the One into whose hands it is a fearful thing to fall. A pastor would be the worst kind of fool to think that he could tamper with God's money. It was said of the sons of Eli just prior to God's announcement of their soon coming deaths in I Samuel; "This sin of the young men was very great in the Lord's sight, for they were treating the Lord's offerings with contempt." (1 Samuel 2:17 NIV)

The events of this era and the collapse of several great men of God was a master plan of Satan to make God's saints fear that it would happen in their church as well. God's faithful pastors know well the consequences of being unfaithful to their calling that is Holy before the Lord. Only a few would dare attempt to betray His trust.

God wants His people to relax in the security of the theocracy. In all of history, even when men have miserably failed in the work of the Lord, God has never seen fit to change His plan. God's plan is still perfectly good; and He still has men who will carry out His plans faithfully and will not dishonor His calling.

God's government must be established in the hearts of God's people. God's people must receive this revelation in order to be blessed to the extent that God desires and intends. We must understand authority in the church.

God's authority always operates in love; however there is a great misunderstanding among God's people regarding love. If there is the least bit of correction involved, some saints begin to say that there is no love; yet God clearly says, "As many as I love, I rebuke and chasten . . . " (Rev. 3:19) God many times uses one of His men to do that correcting. Sometimes as parents, when we must punish our children, whom we love, they may detect anger; but not for one moment has our love for them diminished. We are God's children, and at times we must be corrected for our own good. When a true pastor has been forced to face certain problems head-on, we as God's people must realize the great depth of love that motivates God's overseer to deliver what is needed, rather than what is wanted.

The pastor is the under-shepherd with the responsibility before God for the care of His sheep. Sometimes that care necessitates strong words and bold actions; but such is the role of the man of God in the theocracy.

Due Order

CHAPTER

2

When we pray, we need to pray by the Spirit. God gives us the desires of our hearts. If we are accessible to Him, He implants within our hearts the desires for which He wants us to pray. I received a word from the Lord from a respected man of God in June of 1987, which said, "You must boldly proclaim the words that I'm going to give you."

I began to pray strongly and weep before the Lord, crying out, "Lord, there is a special revelation with which you desire to fill me; and I'm giving birth to it by the Spirit."

For weeks and months I sought the Lord for this revelation, which I knew He wanted to give. One night between Christmas and the New Year of 1988, the Lord awakened me at 3:00 a.m. and said, "Write down all the words that I will speak to you." For several nights the same thing occurred until He had placed within me the revelation of this topic.

Though this is not a new revelation, much of the church has not received it; therefore the progress of the church worldwide has been stifled. In this land of the free because it is a democracy, all of our lives we have been saturated and inundated with democratic thought forms. Because we are democratically oriented, it is very difficult for some Christians to make the mental transition into the THEOCRACY of the church. The enabling of the Spirit is always available to those who desire to do God's will.

The title of this book is, AFTER THE DUE ORDER. There is a definite reason for such a title. The scripture which is the basis for this writing was revealed to me years ago while I was yet in the mainline denominational church of my upbringing. Although I will always love that church, for I found Jesus there, it was the place where I first began to see the utter futility for any church's future if democracy was its form of government. Great tragedy is the outcome sooner or later when men begin to vote on God's business.

God's church is not a democracy. Proverbs 16:25 says, "There is a way that seemeth right unto man, but the end thereof are the ways of death." This proverb can apply in many ways. Physical death can certainly be found there, and so may much more. Unless we approach things after the Spirit, and not after the ways of man in the church, a death grip can take hold of our plans for God and bring them to nothingness. We have seen it over and over again. If it seems right to man, double check!

Many who have never truly understood the church will understand after reading the words of this book. Many are going to see for the first time how God truly desires to operate His church. He has always desired to operate this way; for the Word says that He is the same yesterday, today and forever. God didn't change His mind somewhere along the way about the theocracy. No, men decided they had a better way, they took a vote on it, it passed, and it has been down hill from there.

The Word of God is filled with warnings for us showing the folly of choosing man's leadership over God's direction. What a thrilling day Samuel recounts when at last the ark of God was on its way back home. For years the Philistines had held the ark of God in captivity. Even after it was released, the ark had not come home completely. On this day David's heart was soaring! At last the presence of God would be at home in Israel. He was thrilled! The story of the ark is one of the most serious, yet hilarious, accounts on record of God's dealings with His enemies. The Philistines thought they had the ark of God in captivity, but soon realized that the God of the ark, indeed, had them in captivity.

In I Samuel 5:1-6 we find these words:

"And the Philistines took the ark of God, and brought it from Ebenezer unto Ashdod. When the Philistines took the ark of God, they brought it unto the house of Dagon, and set it by Dagon. And when they of Ashdod arose early on the morrow, behold, Dagon was fallen upon his face to the earth before the ark of the Lord. And they took Dagon, and set him in his place again. And when they arose early on the morrow morning, behold, Dagon was fallen upon his face to the ground before the ark of the Lord; and the head of Dagon and both the palms of his hands were cut off upon the threshold; only the stump of Dagon was left to him. Therefore neither the priest of Dagon, nor any that come into Dagon's house, tread on the threshold of

Dagon in Ashdod unto this day. But the hand of the Lord was heavy upon them of Ashdod, and He destroyed them, and smote them with emerods, even Ashdod and the coasts thereof."

So the Philistines brought up the ark of God which they had captured from God's backslidden people, unto their shrine that was dedicated to the worship of Dagon, a demonic god. They placed the ark, which unknown to them was the dwelling place of the great Holy Spirit, next to the statue of the demonic false deity. The next morning they found the statue lying on the floor face down before the Ark of the Covenant. Not understanding the cause, they set Dagon up again. The following morning, they found him lying on the floor once again. This time both of his hands as well as his head were cut off. God was sending a message to His enemies: "Mess with Me, and heads will roll!" They being dull of spirit, as are all who do not know God, shrugged their shoulders and said, "Huh? Wow! We must have had an earthquake or something!" They completely missed God's first message.

Now we come to verse six, which tops all of the aforementioned warnings. This message was hard to misinterpret; and indeed they got it! "But the hand of the Lord was heavy upon them of Ashdod, and He destroyed them, and smote them with emerods . . . ." The Hebrew term for emerods is *Ophel*, which is "awful" with a long "O". The first meaning of the word is "tumors". The very interesting truth is that these tumors were located in a very precarious place, because they were hemorrhoids. Dake says they were, to put it another way, "swelling piles".

For this malady, the Philistines had made no preparation . . . "H" or otherwise. Their funny and profound conclusion of the whole ordeal was, " . . . The ark of the God of Israel shall not abide with us . . . ." Finally, one might say, they got the message "in the end".

Being the philanthropists that they were, they voted to share these profound blessings with their brothers in Gath; for after quite a quandary over the situation, they answered and said in verse 8, " . . . Let the ark of the God of Israel be carried unto Gath . . . ."

Verse 9 tells us that they carried the ark to Gath; and you guessed it, " . . . the hand of the Lord was against the city with a very great destruction: and He smote the men of the city, both small and great, and they had emerods in their secret parts." We are ever so surprised at the thoughtful solution of the Philistines from Gath, for they voted to send the ark for fellowship with their dear brothers in Ekron. The people of Ekron enjoyed the same divine visitation; and they cried, " . . . They have brought about the ark of the God of Israel to us, to slay us and our people." (What a way to go!)

Now this story lasted seven months. It is a rather difficult thing to imagine the various scenes of life that occurred during that particular period of history. We shall not attempt to do so. We can, however, assume with some confidence that no Don Rickles movie ever surpassed this story for hilarity. I can imagine Heaven roaring with guffaws as this story unfolded. God has a sense of humor. Thank God we are not His enemies!

Chapter six continues the humiliation of the Philistines. After meeting with the pagan priests and the diviners, and asking, " . . . What shall we do to the ark of the Lord? tell us wherewith shall we send it to his place." (I Sam. 6:2) The answer of these pagan pastors was interesting indeed. I Samuel 6:4 asks, " . . . What shall be the trespass offering which we shall return to Him [the God of Israel]?" God has a way of getting people to repent! Their answer was, "five golden mice." These were symbolic, in a very humiliating way, of the five Lords of the Philistines who had all received these blessings alike. Of course the story would not be complete without adding the fact that they also wanted to send "five golden hemorrhoids", which were symbolic, no doubt, of just that.

The story goes on with several more twists and turns, encompassing the entire reign of Saul. The ark never reached its resting place as the center of the worship of Israel until the time of this very important story of the "due order." We find in I Chronicles 15:1-2 these words:

> "And David made him houses in the city of David, and prepared a place for the ark of God, and pitched for it a tent. Then David said, None ought to carry the ark of God but the Levites: for them hath the Lord chosen to carry the ark of God, and to minister unto Him for ever."

This was great wisdom coming out of the mouth of David at a very great price. Indeed, David gleaned this wisdom at the cost of the life of a man named Uzza. In David's zeal without knowledge to bring back the ark of the Lord, he forgot that God is a God of order. Getting out of the order of God always brings death. I Chronicles 13 tells of David zealously sending out the people to get the ark of God without getting God's plan of action. Bad move! Verse 9 and 10 reads as follows:

> "And when they came unto the threshing floor of Chidon, Uzza put forth his hand to hold the ark; for the oxen stumbled. (Now that sounds innocent doesn't it? Any one would have done what Uzza did. He did not want the precious ark of God to fall in the mud.) And the anger of the Lord was kindled against Uzza, and He smote him, because he put his hand to the ark: and there he died before God."

Do you get the idea that God means business? If He says something, He wants it that way; and any disobedience is sin!

David greatly desired to have the presence of the Lord. There was certainly nothing wrong with his motive. To have the presence of the Lord is the desire of any man of God, any true servant of God. However, "There is a way that seemeth right unto a man, but the end thereof are the ways of death." (Pro. 16:25) David's zeal was not ordered in the Spirit, but in the flesh. Tragedy was the outcome. When people who are not in the Spirit try to help out in key situations, the outcome is usually the very same . . . tragic! David's intentions were good; but good intentions mean nothing without God's plan.

Many times people within a congregation see things that apparently need a remedy. They may go to their pastor feeling compelled to instruct him on what needs to be done. Many pastors have fallen by the wayside as they have tried to please men, jumping into any area where anyone sees a need and going beyond their anointed ability. We all must realize that an apparent need does not necessarily mean that it is within God's timing to begin a new program. Why? Because we do not want to be like Uzza; neither do we want to be like David! David surely felt horrible . . . Uzza no longer felt at all. David went about meeting a need in the flesh, and tragedy was the outcome.

Uzza was just obeying orders. He did what any good man would do. At David's command the ark was brought forth. David was God's King and prophet; but he was not acting accordingly, for he failed to get his instructions from God. When the oxen stumbled, Uzza automatically did as any good man would do: he reached up to steady the ark. When he touched it, he died instantly; and it was David's fault! This was indeed a very costly lesson for David to learn. We would do well to learn some lessons from it ourselves.

This is a story of the tragedy that comes from the misuse of delegated authority. Remember, "There is a way that seemeth right unto a man, but the end thereof are the ways of death." Rarely ever has the means justified the end, but it certainly does determine the end. What David wanted was a wonderful thing, however no goal justifies sin. No matter how wonderful a thing we may want, we are never justified to go into sin to get it. Romans 6:23 tells us that " . . . the wages of sin is death . . . ." David sinned in giving Uzza a job which he had no right to do, and Uzza died. The wages of David's sin was the death of another. In our zeal to work for God, we must be very sure we use God's wisdom, prudence and plan, rather than our own. Our ways must always be in accord with the ways of the due order of God. If they are not, they may be successful to some extent; but in the end, they will never reach the glory God intended.

David's zeal for God and His people ended in a nightmare. If the pastor allowed the sheep to have their way in the flock of God without operating after the due order, it would end in a nightmare. When the church tries to serve the Lord, no matter how much love and zeal is involved, without the due order of God, the outcome is always less than victorious. The result of man's work without God's order will never be as glorious as it could have been if done in obedience to God's plan. Uzza's death was directly the result of not operating within the proper framework of the due order and God's delegated authority.

In I Chronicles 15:13 David said, "For because ye did it not at the first, the Lord our God made a breach upon us, for that we sought him not after the due order."

What this shows us is they sought God in a way that God had never ordained. It is true that they were seeking after God, but they sought Him outside of His acceptable terms. Death, in one form or another, comes not only to every man, but to every church as well, which does not seek God after the due order.

In the prophecy given by David Minor, (quoted in the previous chapter), we were told that after the revelation of the government of God was established in the hearts of His people, then the glory would come. The supernatural will be the result of seeking God after the due order. I believe the Lord is saying that any man who is opposed to the theocracy of God will have a problem seeing the supernatural power of God revealed in his life.

Now the question comes, "What is the *DUE ORDER* in the local church today?" Here it is: One God ... One Man! All others to whom authority is delegated under the one man, are to share in both the works and the blessings of God.

We may look at the story of Uzza's death and see that even though David was God's man, his sin resulted in a tragic end for Uzza. The fact that all of God's men are susceptible to human failure has caused many to be afraid to follow a pastor's leading. However, the Bible tells us that we are to learn from the Old Testament. We are to learn from the mistakes recorded there, as well as the successes. Uzza's death was the result of David's tragic mistake of allowing those under himself to be out of control, operating outside their place of spiritual authority.

God's people must function in the place of authority delegated to them. An attempt to function somewhere else will result in death. David allowed Uzza to function in a position where he had no right to be. Uzza died!

Had David as God's prophet first, for he was God's prophet first and Israel's king secondly, directed those delegated under him to function properly and correctly, great life would have been the result instead of death. It was David's fault, not Uzza's; for Uzza was simply obeying orders. David placed him in a position where he should never have been. So it is in the church of the living God today. When men of God operate in the due order of things, and wisely direct and delegate their authority under God, life is the result; and great victory is the effect. But if they do not wisely delegate their authority in God in the congregation, death will be the result. When the leadership of the congregation operates incorrectly, men like Uzza, who are following, try to do things they were not called of God to do; then death comes. Uzza, ill-directed by David, tried to fulfill the Levitical priest's position. He was not of the house of Levi. He was not a priest.

If today, men who are not ministry gifts try to direct the work of the Lord, the work will fail. Ephesians 4:11-12 says:

> "And He gave some, apostles; and some, prophets; and some, evangelists; and some, pastors and teachers; For the perfecting of the saints, for the work of the ministry, for the edifying of the body of Christ:"

Here we are given the fivefold ministry gifts. These are set in the church as gifts from God to the church. The fivefold ministry gifts in the New Testament church correlate with the ministry of the prophets of old. Under the New Covenant, God has ordained five different offices to accomplish the work of leading the New Testament church to maturity and victory. The Old Testament is a type of the New. We may look at the Old Testament and ask how it worked; then, following its typology or pattern, we will see how it works today. The fivefold ministry gifts are the governing body of the church. As we will see, deacons have nothing to do with church government. In the local church the pastor is the governing force directly under the Lord Jesus Christ. God never intended for the church to operate and be governed by the majority vote. Tragedy is always the result when the majority rules rather than God. God has never changed His ways.

Now the question arises, "Who are the fivefold ministry gifts in the church today; and how do they function?" They are to operate within the local church. They are what we have called the "pastor and associate pastors." We have chosen one of the names of these gifts, "pastor", and used it as a general term to describe all the gifts that are resident in the local church. Perhaps this has kept us from understanding that any of the five gifts may be operative in any one of the staff of "pastors". This, of course, will vary with each church according to the grace God has placed in those He has appointed to that congregation. No man chooses what gift he is, that is the business of Jesus alone, Who is Lord of the church.

Because we have used "pastor" as a general term to include all gifts, it has left us wondering, "Where are the apostles, prophets, evangelists and teachers?" Somehow we have gleaned the idea, that out in the congregation, the "flock", are the rest of the ministry gifts. However, those to whom we have referred as "pastors" are the gifts in the local body. The idea that the ability to prophesy makes one a "Prophet", or the ability to teach makes one a "Teacher", is erroneous, just as leading someone to the Lord does not make one an "Evangelist". The Apostle Paul says that we should all desire to prophesy for the edification of the church. Anyone can prophesy who has the Spirit of the Lord, but that does not a "prophet" make. Certainly we should all attempt to lead people to Jesus . . . but that does not an "evangelist" make, nor an "apostle", nor a "pastor", nor a "teacher".

Does this mean that no one in the congregation can ever be called to the fivefold ministry? Certainly not. Where else would God get His ministry gifts? It is always God's best to raise up ministry gifts from within the local church; however, it is important to realize that although one may feel called as a ministry gift, he will never be set in that place in the local church unless God reveals it to the pastor and he recognizes that person as a ministry gift.

In the religious world there has arisen another mistaken assumption that the associate pastoral staff are simply hirelings who answer to the church members. All pastoral staff are ministry gifts themselves, therefore they answer only to the senior pastor in the church. Though we call them "associate pastors" for simplicity's sake, they are indeed ministry gifts who are in the church to assist the pastor, and answer directly to him.

One God, One Man,
No Confusion

CHAPTER

3

God's way, and not man's way, is the way that we must follow. God has always chosen, in His great wisdom, to communicate with the masses through one individual rather than a multitude. He has done this for His own divine reasons; one of which is, no doubt, to avoid confusion. We realize that it is perplexing to hear ten different things from ten different people. Because it is confusing, God has chosen to lead his flock through one man rather than through a multitude. The church is a theocracy.

Theocracy simply means: God rules. One may ask, "What about Proverbs 11:14 that says there is safety in a multitude of counselors? Doesn't that do away with the idea that only one man should be in charge?" Certainly not! We assuredly agree with that scripture. There is safety in a multitude of counselors, or God never would have said it. God has never made any mistakes in the things He has spoken. It does help greatly to have a variety of input and a variety of approaches to solve a problem or answer a question that needs an answer. However, the counselors are given for the purpose of helping the one man that God has called to lead the local church. God never intended for the multitude to lead.

God has already researched man's problem in the area of church government and all other areas. He has given us a flawless plan to redeem man from all of his dilemmas. God in His great wisdom has chosen to do so theocratically. God's formula for success in the church is very simple:

ONE GOD . . . ONE MAN . . . NO CONFUSION.

Jack Hayford, pastor of the great Church On The Way, said in commenting on the subject of democracy as opposed to theocracy, "Any body that has two heads is a freak." Dear ones, I propose to you that the church of the living God was never intended to be a freak. There is only one earthly head, under God, to each local church congregation. God's way has always been One God . . . One Man. The scripture says that God is the same yesterday, today, and forever. In other words, God does not make mistakes. He thought this whole thing through before He ever began. He is the All Wise God.

When God chose to lead between three and six million Jews through the wilderness, God did not choose a senate and a house of representatives, but one man, Moses. The democratic thought process would cry out, "How will you get a balance of power with only one leader?" Let's remember the formula. Remember, God does not make mistakes. ONE GOD . . . ONE MAN . . . NO CONFUSION. We must see that God began things the way He desires to end things. His formula does not produce a lack of accountability. It does not produce imbalance. The formula that God has given to His church is a supernatural formula. The ways of man and God are totally different. The One God . . . One Man formula produces a coalition that absolutely devastates the powers of darkness.

One God . . . One Man in leadership of God's people is the formula. Moses became the man in the equation. Please take note; when Moses died, God did not throw up His hands and say, "OK, you guys were right and I was wrong. We need a multitude of leadership here. Would you vote your leaders in this time, please?"

When Moses, who was the one man in the equation died, God did not get nervous! God did not get upset! God simply moved Joshua, another man, into the formula.

There were three to six million Jews who followed Moses and Joshua in the wilderness; and there were three to six million Jews who were involved in the battles, the spoils and the blessings; but when it came to decision time, ONE GOD and ONE MAN made the decision.

Let's move a few years further into history and look into God's plan in the days of Midian tyranny. Judges 6:1 says:

> "And the children of Israel did evil in the sight of the Lord: and the Lord delivered them into the hand of Midian seven years."

Do you want to know what Israel did to upset God? They voted and decided to do their own thing. They ignored God and democratically decided to handle things their own way. God in His great mercy sought a man to fit into His formula of deliverance for His rebellious people. Judges 6:11-12 says:

> "And there came an angel of the Lord, and sat under

an oak which was in Ophrah, that pertained unto Joash the Abiezrite: and his son Gideon threshed wheat by the winepress to hide it from the Midianites." [Now I want you to get the picture of Gideon in this situation. He was threshing wheat and fearfully trying to hide it from the Midianites.] "And the angel of the Lord appeared unto him, and said unto him, The Lord is with thee, thou mighty man of valour."

Now Gideon heard those words and looked around to see to whom God was speaking, for he knew that surely God was not speaking to him; but no one else was there.

Verse 14 says, "And the Lord looked upon him, and said, Go in this thy might, and thou shalt save Israel from the hand of the Midianites: have not I sent thee?" That last little phrase, "Have not I sent thee?", makes all the difference in the world. If God has sent a man, God will do all that needs to be done. God does not need our ability. God only needs our availability. God does not need our gifts! That's laughable. God is the Gifted One. On one occasion when there was no man available who had sense enough to let God flow through him, God operated through a mule, Balaam's ass. The ass spoke. Again, Jesus answered the Pharisees' request that He rebuke His praising followers by saying, "... I tell you that, if these should hold their peace, the stones would immediately cry out." (Luke 19:40) God has no problem providing a mouthpiece for what He wants to do.

No doubt, all of the aristocrats in Jesus day, upon hearing about John the Baptist who walked around half naked with a camel's hair girdle and eating locust and wild honey, looked upon him as just a little bit offbeat. I Corinthians 1:27 says, however, " . . . God chooses the foolish things of this world to confound the wise . . . " and declares in verse 25, " . . . the foolishness of God is wiser than (the wisdom of) men . . . ." God loves to take some simple thing and use it tremendously, because it proves that God is the One who is doing it anyway.

So here in the sixth chapter of Judges we find Gideon, who is apparently a very timid young man; in fact, he is downright cowardly. He certainly is afraid of the Midianites. If we read the story all the way through, we find that Gideon would definitely not have been chosen by us to be a hero any more than Isaac would have chosen Jacob as his family leader. However, because God's ways are above ours, we will inevitably make mistakes when trusting our fleshly judgements.

What could timid Gideon do? What could a coward accomplish? The answer is that by himself, he could do nothing. However, God had chosen him: God had sent him. That was the all important factor!

Do you remember Peter, the hot-head? the bravado? the man who was quick to use the sword and ask questions later? Was there any hope for Peter? He was a dumb fisherman . . . and yet he was the man Jesus entrusted with the "keys of the kingdom". (Mat. 16:19)

People also asked, " . . . can there any good thing come out of Nazareth? . . . " (John 1:46) Jesus did!

No, we don't operate by man's choice: we operate by God's choice. By himself, Gideon could do nothing; but God chose Gideon. God could look through the mess on the outside and see the heart on the inside. Thank God, He doesn't look at our messes: He looks at our hearts. Gideon started out a coward, but later he became as bold as a lion. Why? When God calls, God also equips. The material with which God begins doesn't matter: when God decides to form and shape, He'll make something useful in His hands.

When the Lord looked upon Gideon and said, "Go in this thy might . . . Have not I sent thee?" Gideon no doubt, thought within himself, "What might?" The might came when God said, "I'm sending you." If God sends you, He'll provide for you everything you need to do the job He has called you to do. ONE GOD . . . ONE MAN. In this case God's one man was Gideon. Verse 16 says, "And the Lord said unto him, Surely I will be with thee, and thou shalt smite the Midianites as one man." AS ONE MAN? Don't forget the formula: One God . . . One Man to lead the people. Once again, God has introduced His man into the equation for victory in the church.

We all remember from childhood the heroic exploits of Gideon and just three hundred of his brave soldiers as they destroyed thousands upon thousands of the Midianites. How? One God . . . One Man: and if you are the man in leadership who is attached to God, that is all that matters. One God and you are a majority.

Folks have asked before, "Where is the God of Gideon?" The God of Gideon is still on the throne, where He has always been. God's side of the formula is always there ready for creative fruitfulness and victory. God's side of the formula is not the problem! The real problem is, "Where are the Gideons of God?"

I will tell you where some of them are. Many of them have allowed themselves to be enchained by the fetters of human opinion. Many are awaiting an end to a committee deadlock. Some are waiting for one filibustering deacon to come around. Why? Because somewhere along the line, men have decided to change the formula to One God . . . One Committee.

Let's go a bit further into history to another time when men, by a majority vote, decided to circumvent the due order of things. They chose to have a man rule over them other than God's man. THEY WANTED TO CHOOSE THEIR OWN MAN. The people said, "OK God, One God . . . One Man; but let it be a man of our choice." No, that won't work either; God has to choose the man. If we try to work God's plan without God's man, catastrophe will be the outcome. They democratically ousted God from the situation, insisting on a man who was not God's choice. While we realize that these Old Testament governments were not democratic governments, we are using the terms dealing with democracy to highlight the choice of man as opposed to the choice of God. They rejected God's man, and by so doing rejected God Himself. God's words to Samuel were, " . . . they have not rejected thee, but they have rejected Me, that I should not reign over them." (I Sam. 8:7) When you reject God's man, you reject God Himself. We'll deal with this further in the next chapter.

The man they wanted was not God's man. Saul was not a spiritual man at all except for evil spirits: but because God saw that their hearts were hardened, He allowed them to have their own way. He allowed majority rule in the decision to have a king. The people said, " . . . make us a king to judge us like all the nations." (I Sam. 8:5) Now doesn't that sound familiar? "But dad, everyone else is doing that." Around our house the typical reply is, "I don't particularly care what everyone else is doing. You are not going to do it!" At this point in the history of these stiff-necked people, God decided to give them the reigns to teach them a very costly lesson.

God will not force you to do anything. I Samuel 10:1 says, "Then Samuel took a vial of oil, and poured it upon his head . . . ." Upon

34

who's head? Saul's. While it was never God's will for them to have an earthly king, still He would not force them to submit to His rule; rather He let them have their own way. God saw that their hearts were wicked. They rejected God's theocracy. They rejected Samuel, and therefore God, because Samuel was God's man. Through Samuel and the prophets God had chosen to direct His people; but the people said they wanted a king like all the other nations. To paraphrase, they said, "Samuel, you are getting old, and we don't trust your sons. When you die, what is going to happen? You had better let us have a king!"

Didn't they know that when Samuel died, God knew how to raise up a prophet to replace him? Did they forget that God was God? They wanted their own way; so Samuel took a bottle of oil and poured it upon Saul's head.

Within the church, when the people of God choose a way other than God's formula, and when God is circumvented by men beginning to vote on the things of God, trouble begins. As we look back at this story, we see trouble beginning in Israel right there. The man God gave them appeared to be just what a human being would want for a king. He was the biggest guy in the country. Their flesh was happy with a fleshly king. However, there was one slight problem: he was a lunatic, as nutty as they come. Once he turned away from God and yielded to his flesh, he became a demoniac. He was stark-raving mad. Power went to his head: that is, the power of darkness went to his head. As the leadership goes, so goes the nation, the business, the church.

Things got dark in Israel, for they had a mad man as king; but now enters the Holy Spirit. He is God's Problem Solver and God's Administrator of the earthly church. Hallelujah! Thank God for Holy Ghost ingenuity as He stepped into this situation. What a thrilling example of God's wisdom is shown here!

Now the Father, Son and Holy Spirit are discussing together how to handle this problem. Perhaps the Holy Spirit said, "They want a king over them? OK, that works for Me. We will give them a king, but he will be our choice and not their choice."

Man always messes things up when he starts voting in the church. We are not talking about voting in our country: praise God for our wonderful national government. The issue here is not the government of a nation, but the government of God's church, of which Israel was a type.

Now in their dilemma, the Spirit of Grace moved to give them their king, but this time he would be a king who was God's prophet. There is no end to God's wisdom: thank God for His mercy. He is willing to come into the messes that we have made and straighten them out. Not only was this man who was the man of God's choosing a prophet; but he was a pastor, a shepherd to a nation, God's man.

Out in the fields all of this time, a young harpist, a shepherd and pastor by nature, is being groomed to lead God's flock. Oh, the wisdom of God! David was God's choice as a king to please the people; but more importantly, David was God's choice as a prophet to please the King of Kings. God has always chosen to lead His flock by one man, who is His choice and not man's. As man looks on the outward appearance, God looks at the heart! David was a shepherd (pastor) with a shepherd's heart. God has always chosen to lead His church through a ministry gift and not a king chosen by the will of the people.

What are the ministry gifts? Apostles, prophets, evangelists, pastors and teachers, these are the five ministry gifts; and they are God's way of leading the church. God told Samuel that when they rejected him, they were rejecting God, because they were choosing their own plan over God's plan. All the way back to the day of David, democracy would not work in the congregation of God's people; and it will not work in the church today.

God graciously chose to interject His man into the formula, outwitting the plan of the flesh and the devil. Great prosperity came to God's people. If we go by God's choice, things will always go better. David was God's choice. It is recorded in II Samuel 5:12 that, " . . . David perceived that the Lord had established him King over Israel . . . ." What a difference it made when God established His man in the place of the people's man! From the time God began to deal with man unto this day, the formula has never ceased to be the same: One God . . . One Man. It is now as it was then. Only the man of God's choice can lead God's people successfully. Many of us have come out of churches where the pastors were "voted in". Most of those churches were filled with death and calamity. On the other hand, if God sends His man, His servant, and says, "You won't vote on this thing. I'm sending My man in here, and he is going to do what I want him to do," then things will work. Only a man called of God can accomplish what God desires. A man uncalled of God, not given to a situation by God, can do nothing but what he can accomplish in the flesh. What any man does in the flesh is worthless. Saul proved that!

God calls pastors as ministry gifts to lead His local church. What exactly is this ministry gift? The Greek word for pastor is *Poimen*, which simply means shepherd. What does the shepherd do? The shepherd leads the flock. He is their provider of food, and their protector and guide. The sheep are given solely into the care of the shepherd. The shepherd does not own them, but he has responsibility for them. Hebrews 13:17 says:

> "Obey them that have the rule over you, and submit yourselves: for they watch for your souls, as they that must give account, that they may do it with joy, and not with grief . . . ."

The shepherd's job is a very heavy job, for he must "give account". Anytime you hear people say, "I wish I had a pastor's easy job," you can just sit back and grin, knowing they are exceptionally ignorant of the facts. Only God can give a shepherd a shepherd's heart; and only God can place a shepherd within a flock and make him successful. One God . . . One Man . . . God's Man!

The pastor's job is far from a life of leisure that can be done on the golf course in the afternoons. Neither is it a job where he may run himself ragged with the cares of life, becoming too tired when he comes in at evening, and too tired to rise up early in the morning, to seek the face of God. Constant vigilance must be kept in the Spirit. Only men of prayer are truly successful.

There are wolves in sheep's clothing on every hand; and many times sheep do not recognize wolves until it is too late. God has given the pastor the job of thwarting wolves. John 10:12-13 reads:

> "But he that is an hireling, and not the shepherd, whose own the sheep are not, seeth the wolf coming, and leaveth the sheep, and fleeth: and the wolf catcheth

them, and scattereth the sheep. The hireling fleeth, because he is an hireling, and careth not for the sheep."

Now if the pastor is a hireling, he could not care less about what happens to the sheep. Sometimes the job of the shepherd is not a popular one; but a true shepherd will not allow any wolf in sheep's clothing to come among his sheep. It is extremely frustrating when the shepherd lays down his life to rid the sheep of wolves, and the sheep accuse him of being unloving. Acts 20:28-30 says:

> "Take heed therefore unto yourselves, and to all the flock, over the which the Holy Ghost hath made you overseers, to feed the church of God, which he hath purchased with His own blood. For I know this, that after my departing shall grievous wolves enter in among you, not sparing the flock. Also of your own selves shall men arise, speaking perverse things, to draw away disciples unto them."

Sometimes the duty of the pastor/shepherd is very unpleasant; because from the very flock of God that the pastor loves, wolves appear. The Lord spoke to my wife something that I shall never forget as she inquired of Him concerning the emergence of a wolf among the flock. Listen to the words of the Lord, for He said, "A wolf in sheep's clothing may simply be any sheep who will open himself to the wolf." The transformation from sheep to wolf is no hard thing: it can be accomplished by any sheep allowing entrance to the wolf (Satan). If you fellowship with wolves, you are in danger of becoming one yourself; for it's the spirit of the wolf which seeks to attach itself and destroy the sheep. You become like those with whom you fellowship. Paul warns in I Cor. 15:33, "Do not be misled: 'Bad company corrupts good character.'" (NIV) If you fellowship with wolves, the first sign is that you will begin to smell like one, and then you will begin to think like one, and before you know it you will have become a wolf. For your own good, the next step needs to be the shepherd's rod applied to your head. God has given the shepherd to protect the sheep from the wolf: it is the duty of the true shepherd to use the rod. Jesus said,

" . . . the good shepherd giveth his life for the sheep." (John 10:11). It is no fun thing to fight off a pack of wolves; but the Chief Shepherd will not tolerate wolves in His flock. The pastor's job is to carry out the desires of the Chief Shepherd, Jesus Christ.

One God . . . One Man, is the pattern followed by the Lord of the church. It was so in the beginning, and so it is today. In this democracy in which we live, it is very difficult for some to make that switch out of the democratic thought process and into the theocracy of the church. Now, however, in the end of the world, God's theocracy is beginning to be reestablished as never before in the hearts of God's people.

David had his mighty men who gave him their input and wisdom, but David was the man with the responsibility before God. Because of that fact, David stood before the Lord for the decisions he made. Neither Jonathan or David's mighty men were required to answer for David's decisions. David did! The same is true today: the one God places in authority is the one who must give an account.

God has set in the church apostles, prophets, evangelists, pastors and teachers to govern the church. When it comes down to the bottom line, the responsibility is upon the senior pastor. Should he allow the whole congregation to have their democratic say in the affairs of the church, it would still be the pastor's fault when things went wrong. God has a very definite reason for His One God . . . One Man formula.

The Local Church/Deacons

CHAPTER

4

Throughout twenty years of preaching the gospel, there has been a particular passage of scripture which has been of great interest to me. Thanks to religious preaching and teaching, many have totally misunderstood and misconstrued this text, professing that it means something it does not. This passage is found in the sixth chapter of Acts. Its application has probably become one of the greatest errors to have been taught in the church regarding church government. In this chapter we will examine this text verse by verse.

As I was reading from a book by a great pastor, a statement he made caught my attention. He said, in effect, that every church was a unique body of unique individuals, all put together in a unique place, for a unique purpose. This being true, the principles of church government will be applied with a little different slant, depending upon the abilities and needs of the particular pastor, as well as the strengths and weaknesses within the congregation. This does not mean that the principles are changed; but by necessity they must be applied a bit differently, depending upon the characteristics of each unique congregation.

We make a mistake in the very beginning if we look to the sixth chapter of Acts for a text dealing with church government. It does not. When we take the sixth chapter of Acts, falsely assuming that it is the guiding text for church governmental selection, and compound that error by applying each verse legalistically to the already erroneous selection process of officials, things really get flaky! Let's look at Acts 6 together:

"And in those days, when the number of the disciples was multiplied, there arose a murmuring of the Grecians against the Hebrews, because their widows were neglected in the daily ministration. Then the twelve called the multitude of the disciples unto them, and said, It is not reason that we should leave the word of God, and serve tables. Wherefore, brethren, look ye out among you seven men of honest report, full of the Holy Ghost and wisdom, whom we may appoint over this business. But we will give ourselves continually to prayer, and to the ministry of the word. And the saying pleased the whole multitude: and they chose Stephen, a man full of faith and of the Holy Ghost, and Philip, and Prochorus, and Nicanor, and Timon, and Parmenas, and Nicolas a proselyte of Antioch: Whom they set before the Apostles: and when they had prayed, they laid their hands on them. And the word of God increased; and the number of disciples multiplied in Jerusalem greatly; and a great company of priests were obedient to the faith." Acts 6:1-7

Here we see a problem arose because the Hebrew widows were being overlooked in the daily distribution of food. The twelve gathered all the disciples together and said that it would not be right for them [the twelve] to neglect the ministry of the Word of God in order to wait on tables. They then gave instruction to the other disciples to choose from among them seven individuals who were qualified to handle the matter. They further stressed their duty to give themselves over to prayer and the ministry of the Word. The proposal made the whole group happy; and they then chose Stephen and Philip, Prochorus and Nicanor, Timon and Parmenas, as well as Nicholas. These men were presented to the Apostles who, after prayer, laid their hands on them and released them to carry out the administration of this particular problem. These men were called deacons.

The term *deacon* means "servant". The deacon is to serve primarily two entities: number one, of course, is God; and number two, the deacon is to serve the pastor (ministry gift). The foremost duty of the deacon in the local church is to serve the pastor by carrying out such services as are required by God in His church, under the authority He has established in the pastor.

Ministry gifts are these: apostles, prophets, evangelists, pastors and teachers. Among these gifts there are varying degrees of authority. While each of these ministry gifts may be operative on the local level, this is not always the case. A small church may have only a pastor, while a larger church may have a man doing the work of a pastor who may actually stand in the office of apostle; and under his authority there may be any number of the other ministry gifts. Whether many or few, those given to the local church have authority only within that local body; and they must be recognized by the senior pastor.

God has also given ministry gifts for the oversight of the worldwide church. As God elevates these men to the position of His choosing, their gifts to the body of Christ begin to be recognized and received beyond the local church. It is important to note at this point, that these men or women only function as ministry gifts to those who receive them as an apostle, prophet, evangelist, pastor or teacher. The Holy Spirit may have them serving in a variety of ways. They may be called to pastor a local church; and at the same time, have the oversight of other pastors. While in the local church, the senior pastor must carry the authority and responsibility for all those under him; he also needs someone to whom he may submit. Yes, Jesus is his Lord; but the local pastor also needs a pastor for counsel, for advice, and also for comfort.

There are ministry gifts for the world, and there are also ministry gifts for just the local church. At Cornerstone Faith Center, I am the senior pastor; however I do the work of an apostle because the Holy Spirit sent me to do so in establishing this particular congregation. The term *apostle* literally means, "one sent forth" by God to lay the gospel foundation for the church. While there were only twelve "Apostles of the Lamb", God continues to give the ministry gift of apostle to His church. Within the New Testament we find several men other than the Twelve who were called apostles: Barnabas (Acts 14:4,14), Andronicus and Junias (Romans 16:7), two unnamed brethren (II Cor. 8:23), Epaphroditus (Philippians 2:25), Paul, Silas and Timothy (I Thess. 2:6). I am an apostle to this local church by the direction of the Holy Spirit, just as someone like Lester Sumrall is received by people around the world as an apostle. The Holy Spirit has confirmed the worldwide apostolic calling that is upon Brother Sumrall's life by the work he has done in establishing churches around the world. Those sent to hold any of these offices must do the work that is required. The Apostle Paul, in defending his apostleship to the Corinthian church said:

> " . . . Am I not an apostle? . . . Are you not the result
> of my work in the Lord. Even though I may not be an
> apostle to others, surely I am to you! For you are the
> seal of my apostleship in the Lord." I Cor. 9:1-2 (NIV)

We find another example in Paul's instruction to Timothy to, " . . . do the work of an evangelist . . . ." (II Tim. 4:5 NIV) Please understand that these titles are being used to explain God's flow of authority: I take no pride in titles, and I am confident that I may speak for all God's servants who only wish to be found faithful to the call God has given.

I serve as the senior pastor in this local church; and working by my side are other pastors given to this local body. They, too, are ministry gifts, operating under the authority of the senior pastor. In the local church, the senior pastor is over all other ministry gifts resident within that congregation.

However, because God has given apostles, prophets, evangelists, pastors and teachers, who have been elevated positionally by the Lord of the church to serve above the local ministry, I submit myself to them in the Lord. As a local pastor, I have a pastor that God has given me to whom I submit for instruction and correction.

In the local church, the deacon submits himself and serves the Lord, as a servant to the pastor of the church. The Greek word for deacon is *diakonos*. Strongs Exhaustive Concordance of the Bible says, "The word *diakonos* or deacon is used in the New Testament as a technical term alongside of the word, *Episcopos*." The word *episcopos* refers to the government of the church. In the New Testament the words pastor, elder, bishop, shepherd and overseers refer to ministry gifts. New Testament elders were not elected by a congregation, but appointed by God through apostolic placement. Please notice that the word *deacon* is used "alongside of" a leader or ministry gift. According to Ephesians 4:11, a ministry gift is a person whom God has set in the church as a gift from Himself. If a man or woman is a ministry gift from God, set into a local church, he must be recognized as such by the local pastor. If the local pastor, being a true man of God, does not recognize an individual in any of these areas of leadership, then that individual is not sent as a ministry gift to that congregation. A ministry gift is almost always a person who gives his full time to the work of the Lord.

Some may wonder if they are ministry gifts. Perhaps the call is there but the time is not yet. If you are called as a ministry gift, you still must be equipped, and you still must be sent forth. There is a three-fold plan to being used of God as a ministry gift: the Calling, the Equipping, and the Sending Forth. Many heard the call and went, only to fail, because they had not been equipped; and they had not yet been sent. When God is ready for your service as a ministry gift to begin, you will be successful if you are faithful to the call. You will not need to assert yourself, for you will be recognized as a gift from God. When the time comes that you are recognized as a gift from God to the church, in most cases your livelihood will be supplied by the church.

Please remember that the *diakonos* or *deacon* is "called alongside of" a leader. The term *deacon* is not a title given to a group of people who are to govern the church; rather it describes those who are called as servants or helpers to the fivefold ministry gifts. The deacon is to help and serve the ministry gift in the work of the church. Ephesians 6:21 is a wonderful example of how the deacon (Tychicus) served the ministry gift (Paul):

> "But that ye also may know my affairs, and how I do, Tychicus, a beloved brother and faithful minister in the Lord, shall make known to you all things."

King James says that Tychicus was a faithful "minister" in the Lord. In our terminology today, the word *minister* has a totally different connotation than it did in Jesus' day, and in the day of Paul. In that day the word *minister* simply meant a servant. The King James version says that Tychicus was a minister to Paul; therefore we might simply think that he was a fellow minister: but we would be wrong! The Americanization of King James terminology leads to error in most cases. The New International Version says, "faithful servant". The Greek says "Tychicus my faithful *diakonos* (deacon, servant)." Tychicus was a personal deacon and servant to Paul, the ministry gift. He was not Paul's overseer but a faithful servant carrying out the menial matters of Paul's ministry, so that Paul could walk in the Spirit and carry out the weightier things which God had called him to accomplish for the kingdom.

Paul sent Tychicus, his faithful servant (deacon), to tell the Ephesian church how Paul was doing. As a ministry gift, Paul had an entourage of faithful servants, who helped him in menial matters. The Greek says plainly that "deacon" means "one who helps in menial matters."

All Christians are servants of God; therefore all Christians are "deacons", in the sense that they serve God. The pastor is certainly a "deacon", in that he serves the Lord; and he also serves the people. The serving of food was the original purpose of deacons in the New Testament church. They served literal groceries, while the pastor serves spiritual nourishment. So, in a general sense, we are all "deacons"; but in a very literal sense, Tychicus was a servant of the Apostle Paul, the ministry gift.

We are all serving as a *diakonos* in one way or another. Though we may differ as to office and placement in the body of Christ, all Christians are servants of God. God puts different folks into differing positions in the body; however the good news is that God is great about giving us promotions. Jesus taught us in the parable of the talents (Luke 19:12-27) that He rewards those who are faithful when only a little is entrusted to them. His words were:

> "And he said unto him, 'Well, thou good servant:
> because thou hast been faithful in a very little, have
> thou authority over ten cities.'" Luke 19:17

God will move us up in rank as we are faithful to fulfill what He has given us to do presently. God is the Author of "fair business practices."

The most efficient and productive manner of service in the kingdom of God is to find out and recognize where you fit in the scope of God's kingdom. The fastest way for you to get a promotion in the kingdom, is to serve the delegated authority of God that is over you. For instance, if you are an usher in the church, you should serve the head usher with all your strength. A Sunday school teacher should serve the Sunday school superintendent with all he has. The choir should flow with all their hearts with the director. Eventually, those who serve faithfully where they are will be recognized and promoted. If you as an usher, teacher or singer want to know how to be the very best servant of God that you can possibly be, then serve those over you with all your might. In so doing, you are serving God with all your might; and God, Who is the promoting One, will be well pleased with your life. What ever you do in the church, do it with all your heart. Realize that serving the head usher is serving the Lord. Serving the Sunday school superintendent is serving the Lord. If you try to serve the Lord, Who is the world's greatest Proponent of excellence in all things, and do a sloppy job of serving those under whose authority He has placed you, you will never be promoted. You will always feel unfinished in your ambitions for God. However, if you will embrace this simple truth, that the way to serve God is to properly relate to the delegated authority under whom you serve, you will be on your way to successful and fruitful service to the Lord. THE WAY WE SERVE THE FATHER IS BY PROPERLY RELATING TO HIS DELE-GATED AUTHORITY UNDER WHICH WE SERVE. No one can bypass the delegated authority of God and be pleasing to Him. You can go straight to God in prayer and in your personal needs, but you can never bypass authority to be a spiritual "lone ranger" and properly fit into God's plan to use you in His church.

There are many "super saints" who have been in the churches for years. Sadly, they think they have all the answers; but in reality they know so little. Church attendance does not guarantee great wisdom and knowledge in spiritual matters. A spiritual hermit, not called as a ministry gift, yet full of self supposed knowledge, will feel they do not need the body of Christ or a pastor. Someone in this condition has never learned the first principle of serving God: submitting to His delegated authority. Should you find someone who wants to con-stantly be giving a word from the Lord, yet submits to no one, my recommendation is that you flee this kind of person on sight. They can never truthfully relate to God because He is a God of order; therefore their power is dangerous. You should not flow in their direction lest you, too, be led astray. In order to serve God successfully we must all learn to be servants. Without that knowledge, we cannot serve the Lord as He would have us serve Him. If we never serve, we can never lead!

I had to learn that lesson years ago. I had finished college and ministered successfully, as men see success, in several churches. I had served the Lord in other lands, seeing thousands come to Him, before I learned the lesson of servanthood. The blessings of God can come to those for a time who do not know how to serve; but those blessings will be limited, and life will turn into calamity if the lesson of servanthood does not eventually surface in our ministry.

After serving successfully at the First Christian Church in Aberdeen, Mississippi, I received the baptism in the Holy Spirit and the "left foot of fellowship" almost simultaneously. Leaving there, my wife and I were forced to start all over in the things of God. I had been the senior pastor in every church I had served and had seen great success as a preacher in a church that boldly proclaims the new birth, but does not accept the baptism in the Holy Spirit for believers today.

Leaving that denomination, the Lord took us to Canton, Georgia, where I was to serve as an associate pastor for the first time in my life. There I was to learn the great lesson of being a servant under a former Methodist minister. To a preacher of the Christian Church denomination, submitting to a Methodist was like a cat in submission to a mouse, or a professor in submission to a freshman. Spiritual pride had to go, and go it did; but not without great turmoil in the process.

Charles Davis, a wonderful man of God, and the pastor of Canton Community Church of Canton, Georgia, whom I dearly love and appreciate in the Lord, was the senior pastor and my boss. He asked me to do things I was not accustomed to doing . . . things I detested doing. However, after much complaining to the Lord about how I should not have to do those things as His servant, I began to understand that you cannot be a servant of God, without first being a servant to those under whose authority He has placed you. The Lord very plainly told me that I should not be concerned with the things I was asked to do; rather I should learn to be a servant. The word of the Lord came unto me saying, "Submit yourself to the older man, and in due season I will raise you up." I Peter 5:5,6 reads:

> "Likewise, ye younger, submit yourself unto the elder . . . for God resisteth the proud, and giveth grace to the humble. Humble yourselves therefore under the mighty hand of God, that he may exalt you in due time . . . ."

I said, "Yes Sir!" Having asked Charles what he wanted me to do, I set about doing it and refused to complain. He wanted me to go out and knock on doors and evangelize. That was not my understanding of how God added to the church daily; and for the most part, house to house evangelization is still not my "cup of tea". However, the theological correctness of the situation was not what God was interested in teaching me. I got the feeling that had Charles wanted me to jump off a cliff, God would not disagree. Why? The lesson was "How to be a Servant". I desperately needed to learn how to serve another without complaining.

I hit every house I could see. I knocked on the doors in Jesus' name. As far as I know, I accomplished not one eternal thing . . . with the great exception of this: I learned to be a servant. That lesson through the years has been invaluable, without price. For without that lesson safely under the belt, no one can successfully serve our King. If we want to be used of God, we must learn what it means to be a servant. We must find our place in the body of Christ, and with a heart full of gladness, with the fullest extent of our ability, serve those who are over us in the Lord. Many want to be leaders who have never learned to serve. That desire might as well be forgotten. A leader who has never learned to serve will be a self-serving dictator. You cannot properly lead if you have not been a servant.

The Greek language pointedly says that the deacon (*diakonos*) was one who assisted by serving the ministry gift. In no way did the deacon rule the church. The job of the deacon had nothing to do with church government. He served the ministry gifts, who were themselves the governing agents of the church, by reason of the fact that they were assigned to that task by God.

A tradition of man has arisen based on the choosing of servants or deacons in Acts 6 which asserts that because these men were to take care of a material need, the modern day deacon should therefore oversee church finances and all church business; for after all, does the Word not say, "Whom we may appoint over this business?" (Acts 6:3)

Acts 6:1 tells us of the particular business referred to in this scripture. Was it a building program, or church finances, or foreign missions? No! What business were they to handle?

> "In those days when the number of the disciples was increasing, and the Grecian Jews among them complained against the Hebraic Jews because their wid-

ows were being overlooked in the daily distribution of
food . . . ." (NIV)

So we see the business referred to in Acts 6:1 was the distribution
of food and nothing more. To glean from that scripture that it was
God's will for the deacons to take charge of all church business is a
pure example of theological absurdity. That, however, is what is
being taught in many denominations. It is fallacious by definition to
believe such teaching, for the deacon was a server and not a ruler.

Now let's look at what can happen when a deacon (*diakonos/
servant*) does exactly that with all his heart! Acts 6:5 says, "And they
chose Stephen." What was Stephen chosen to do? He was chosen to
be a servant, a grocery carrier. He distributed food to the Greek
speaking widows in the church; but he served the Lord with all his
heart. Verse 8 reads, "But Stephen, full of faith and power did great
wonders among the people." What happened? God observed a young
man with a right heart and looked over to the Lord Jesus and said,
"There's one we can promote!" God anointed him with great power
and might; and Stephen went from being a menial servant distributing
food, to become a great evangelist for the Lord. He was anointed with
the Holy Spirit's ability. Miracles, signs and wonders were the result
of a young man faithfully serving God as a servant. I seriously doubt
if we ever would have read such glorious details of Stephen, had he
considered himself too superior to be a servant.

In the church the deacon is to serve the ministry gift. You need to
serve the one who is your immediate overseer in the things of God. If
you will do so with all your heart, one day soon you may be spoken
of like Stephen of old. It will work the same today as then; for God
is the same yesterday, today, and forever.

Let it be clearly understood, however, that the job of the deacon has
nothing to do with church finances. In fact, the pastor alone stands in
judgement for God's money. If things go wrong, God comes to the
pastor and confronts him and no other. If the pastor is accountable
before God, having the responsibility for it, then he should also have
the direction of it. Finances are indicative of ruling. The distribution
of funds and ministry are absolutely tied together, hand in hand. If the
pastor, as God's ministry gift to the church, does not have the final say

in financial matters, he is a servant to those who do have that final say; and the church is once more a democracy.

One fellow said to me, "Pastor, I don't believe the church is a democracy. I believe it should be run by presbyters." If more than one presbyter is running the church, you still have democracy. If there is more than one head, you are in a democracy any way you shake it.

Many say, "We believe in a plurality of elders." Good! So do I. However I don't believe, nor does the Bible teach, that God desires a plurality of headship. We have a plurality of elders in our church. Every pastor in the church is an elder; but the terms *elder* and *pastor* are synonymous, meaning those given the oversight of God's flock. There is only one head of the church on earth, however, and that is the senior pastor under the Lordship of Jesus the True Head of the Church.

You may wonder if this contradicts the truth of Proverbs 11:14b which states, " . . . in the multitude of counsellors there is safety." There is no contradiction here: this is an important place to apply that wisdom. Though the pastor has the final decision, he should be wise enough to have a plurality of advisers giving him input for those decisions. I personally have an advisory board made up of congrgational members and my pastoral staff, who give me input and wisdom from their fields of expertise in matters where it is needed.

Whenever there is a decision of major proportions to be made in the church, I call them together and ask their feelings on the subject. I weigh their wisdom and advice, and then pray. This allows me to broaden my understanding through the men God has given me as I listen for God's direction. Still, the final decision is ultimately mine as the pastor.

When Acts 6:3 says, "That we may put them in charge of this business . . . ", it refers only to an isolated case in which a need arose for servants to handle the problems of the Grecian widows. It in no way refers to any other business, nor is it in any way a proof text showing us that deacons are to run church business.

In reference to church finances, Acts 4:35 records that they were laid at the apostles feet for distribution. Who were the apostles? Ministry gifts given by God! So today, the pastor must oversee the finances of the church. Again in Acts 5 we find the story of Ananias and Sapphira, who were lying to the church, the apostles, and most importantly to the

Holy Spirit. Yet we can learn a lesson from them, for though they were trying to deceive, they followed the due order of things; for we read that they sold a piece of property, keeping back part for themselves, ". . . and brought a certain part and laid it at the apostles feet." (Acts 5:2b) So again we see that from the beginning of the evolving church, it was indeed established that the finances of the church were to be directly under the authority of the local heads of the church.

Always the ministry gifts have governed the church. Today's church is much more mature than the infant church in Acts 6. At that stage of church development, the only ministry gifts were the apostles. We have no written proof of any other leadership to this point, for the church was in its infancy: and the apostles were doing it all. They were the pastors or overseers of the church. We know that they had a tremendously large flock, for 3000 were born again in Acts 2. Only a few days later, 5000 more were added; "And the Lord added to the church daily such as should be saved." (Acts 2:47b) The Lord Jesus had ascended into heaven only twelve months earlier. The church began in A.D. 30; and these events recorded in Acts 6 occurred in A.D. 31. The church is a one year old baby church. The Apostles of the Lamb, the pastors of the church, are one year old in the Lord's Spirit.

Those espousing democracy in the church generally believe that God did something supernatural in the infant church that He will no longer do for us today. It is taught that the twelve Apostles of the Lamb were super-saints, men who walked in a place with God that is unattainable to us today. However, while these men were highly honored to have served on the earth with our Precious Lord, the fact remains that they were men just as we. The church and its leaders were only one year in age at this time. How many of us would think it wisdom to pattern our lives after one year old children to any great extent? Still, traditional religion says to us that we need to be very careful to read the 6th chapter of Acts, and legalistically use it to establish a form of church government. My friend, this is wrong thinking! To assume that Acts 6 is God's proof text for democracy in the church is a major theological error.

In the light of the fact that major Christian leaders have fallen prey to their own lust of late, and that the national news media are doing all they can to make America distrust anyone who is a servant of the Lord, the Spirit of God spoke to me a scripture. Never before had I seen this verse in this light, until it was revealed to me by the Spirit. John 6:28 reads, "Then said they unto Him, What shall we do, that we might work the works of God?"

Have you ever asked that question? God, what must I do to see the glory? What must I do to bring Heaven down? What must I do to have my prayers answered? What must I do to end this seeming impotence in my Christian life? I believe in miracles and the supernatural; so what must I do to see it? Jesus answered all of our questions with these words:

> "This is the work of God, that ye believe on him
> whom He hath sent." (John 6:29)

Do we want to do the work of God? What Jesus was saying to those people, was in essence, "You say you want to do the works of God, but have no idea what they are, and have never yet even begun to do them." The Father had sent Jesus to them, He said the work of God is to believe in the one whom God has sent.

Jesus' earthly ministry ended nearly 2,000 years ago, but God still sends His men into the world with His message of life. It is no surprise that Satan's plan is to make Christians distrust their pastors, the one God has sent for them. Most of that distrust is around the subject of money. The truth of the matter is, folks who want to control the money they give to God, have never truly given it. When you give something, you also give up the control of the gift. A believer with a true heart will joyfully give his money to God, and then trust God alone to tell the pastor where to put it.

Jesus said the work of God is to believe in the one God sent to you. Of course we understand that this means first of all to believe in Jesus' saving work. However, it is also essential for you to trust and follow the pastor God has sent to lead you. If you don't, why in the world would you attend that church?

I believe the fall of the very well known servants of God of late was a master plan of Satan to plant doubt and distrust in the hearts of God's people toward their leaders. It makes no difference what the world thinks, but if God's people pull away from their God given leaders,

Satan will have won a great victory.

If you want to see miracles and supernatural occurrences, you must first do the work of God, which is believing in the one God has sent you. The beginning of the work of God is to accept God's authority in the one God sent to you. If you will believe in the one God sent to lead you (your pastor), and be faithful where you are as a servant, doing all that is within you to help those over you in the Lord to achieve their God given goals, God will raise you up and bless you to achieve more than you could ever dream.

Acts 6: Model or Momentary Method?

CHAPTER

5

Acts 6:1-7 reads:

> "In those days when the number of disciples was increasing, the Grecian Jews among them complained against the Hebraic Jews because their widows were being overlooked in the daily distribution of food. So the Twelve gathered all the disciples together and said, 'It would not be right for us to neglect the ministry of the word of God in order to wait on tables. Brothers, choose seven men from among you who are known to be full of the Spirit and wisdom. We will turn this responsibility over to them and will give our attention to prayer and the ministry of the word.' This proposal pleased the whole group. They chose Stephen, a man full of faith and of the Holy Spirit; also Philip, Prochorus, Nicanor, Timon, Parmenas, and Nicolas from Antioch, a convert to Judaism. They presented these men to the apostles, who prayed and laid their hands on them. So the word of God spread. The number of disciples in Jerusalem increased rapidly, and a large number of priests became obedient to the faith." (NIV)

I believe with all of my heart, that the Lord's desire is that the sixth chapter of Acts be viewed, not as our standard for governmental selection in the church, but as an illustration of how very ingenious the Holy Spirit of God was and is. All with which He had to deal in the beginning of the church were thousands and thousands of infants, including the leaders (pastors, overseers). They were all baby Christians. His top leaders were only a year old in the Spirit of God. Remember, the New Testament, for the most part, had not yet even been written. The church began in A.D. 30, and this story takes place probably very close to A.D. 31; therefore the greatest of them are babes in Christ.

There was a problem of administration in the infant church. The Greek speaking Jews complained that the Hebrew speaking Jews were neglecting to give them their fair share of food. At that time there were Jews gathered from all over the world. Many of them had become a part of the church. While this was a time of immaturity in the church, it was also a time of great zeal. When those two elements are merged into one, they normally equal TROUBLE.

The church had all things in common. Let's look at Acts 4:34-37:

> "Neither was there any among them that lacked: for as many as were possessors of lands or houses sold them, and brought the prices of the things that were sold, And laid them down at the apostles' feet: and distribution was made to every man according as he had need. And Joses, who by the apostles was sur-named Barnabas, (which is, being interpreted, the son of consolation,) a Levite, and of the country of Cy-press, having land, sold it, and brought the money, and laid it at the apostles' feet."

Here is the picture: the Holy Spirit has thousands of baby Christians brand new, one year old in the Lord. They were not just baby Christians like many of today's "laid back" Christians. These are baby "charismatics". They are in the proverbial stage of the "straight jacket". There is a time when people newly filled with the Spirit need to be somewhat controlled and corralled.

In fact, one day just after my wife and I had received the baptism of the Holy Spirit, the Lord spoke to me saying, "Shut up", in those very words. He also told me that I was doing more harm than good and should relax and let Him work through me in His own way.

In commenting on these new babes in Christ having all things in common, Finis Dake, a renowned scholar of the Word, says, "The community of goods was never practical nor was it a Biblical ordinance." In fact, the only time you find that communal reference in the Bible is here in Acts 4:35, which is a history of the infant church. The probable reason that it appears there, is that it is recording the deeds of a group of very zealous babes in Christ.

God was dealing with an infant church, which was feeling its way along. Even the apostles were learning as this wonderful age was being ushered in. This is not to say that God was not doing a supernatural work in them: He certainly was! However, the fact remains that He was doing a supernatural work in one year old Christians; and there is a limit to how much you can do in a one year old. I think we make a mistake if we take too far the work of God in these men, who were men even as we.

Acts 6:2,3 reads, "Then the twelve called the multitude of the disciples unto them." Matthew Henry, a renowned Bible scholar, says the term *multitude* here meant the principal leaders of the Jewish people.

So the twelve apostles have called to them the leaders of the Jewish neighborhoods, prominent people in the community, who knew the people well. The church at this time was already very large. There were literally thousands of new Christians. The apostles could not possibly have known them all, and certainly not well enough to select men of character for this job. I don't have thousands upon thousands in my congregation; but even with those I have, I don't know the heart and character of each of them. The apostles certainly would not have known their flocks on a personal basis. Therefore the apostles called the *multitude* of prominent people and leaders together to help find seven men who could handle the problem of the grocery distribution.

Assuming that this passage of scripture was given for a pattern, teaching us how to democratically select church government, can you imagine the nomination problem? There were no TV personalities, no newspaper reporters, not even a Republican or Democratic chairperson. Chaos would be the order of the day!

This, however, is not a governmental selection procedure. Nevertheless, that is what many have taught in traditional churches. No, the apostles called the leading Jewish saints, who knew the people in the community, to help them find the good men needed. Remember, this church has twelve pastors, and at least that many thousands of members. Three thousand were added on the Day of Pentecost, five thousand a few days later, then we read, " . . . the Lord added to the church daily . . . ." (Acts 2:47) I don't believe for one moment that only one per day, adding up to 365 were added in this first year of the exploding baby church. There were thousands upon thousands coming to Jesus. Therefore, it is easily understood that as the apostles were trying to do the work of the ministry in overseeing the growing flock, they could have become overwhelmed without help. Finally they threw up their hands and said, "Go get us some help!"

The apostles are not dealing with the entire huge church in these verses. They are dealing with a number of prominent leaders, referred to as a multitude. The need here is simply for a few good men to do a job. Deacons are servants who do those tasks which are needful in order to help free the ministry gifts. They needed the leaders to help them find good men of character to be of service.

Now in verse three, it is clearly seen that the apostles were the ones who appointed these men as deacons, and not the congregation.

> "Then the twelve [apostles] called the multitude of the disciples unto them, and said; It is not reason that we [the apostles] should leave the word of God and serve tables. Wherefore, brethren, look ye out among you seven men of honest report, full of the Holy Ghost and wisdom, whom we [the apostles] may appoint over this business." *(brackets added)*

Who appointed them? The apostles! Here is what happened: the apostles said, "We will appoint some men to take care of this matter, but we don't have time to go out among the thousands and find the men. Would you please help us?"

They are not here espousing any governmental selection process. There is a need for help in handling this particular, isolated incident. They are looking for some good servants.

If we will follow the thought of the theocratic church throughout the whole Bible, then we will understand that the ministry gifts must always appoint all such individuals. This must be so; for the church has been theocratic, and not democratic, from its inception. God is not inconsistent! He did not in the 6th chapter of Acts blend democracy with theocracy. Any time the minds of men get involved and begin to vote, God's wisdom is simply removed from the scene.

So the multitude that was called together in verse 2 was the smaller group of prominent Jewish leaders. It was to them the apostles appealed for help in finding the personnel to handle the distribution problem. These prominent Jewish leaders were used as sounding boards by the apostles to find "seven men of honest report, full of the Holy Ghost and wisdom." (Acts 6:3)

Please notice the wording in verse 5, "And the saying pleased the whole multitude." Verse 2 reads "the multitude"; and verse 5 reads "the whole multitude". Therefore, we can see that "the multitude" referred to a selection committee, called together by the apostles, and not the "whole multitude" as distinguished in verse 5.

We must realize that this was simply one isolated case, which was wisely handled in this way at this particular time. However, it is not a text which we must legalistically apply to the church government today.

Why then, do we read, "the saying pleased the whole multitude"? It was not because the vote went their way, for no voting occurred. They were pleased because they felt secure in the fact that God's men were hearing from God in how to lead them. They said upon hearing it, "Yes, that is God!"; and they were pleased.

Verse 6 reads, "Whom they set before the apostles: and when they had prayed, they laid their hands on them." Tradition tells us that this verse is simply depicting a religious ceremony. We have all seen them over and over again in our churches' little religious ceremonies, called ordination of elders and deacons. While there may be nothing inherently wrong with our ceremonies, we must heed Jesus' warning that the Word of God can be made of none effect through men's traditions. (See Mark 7:13)

False tradition tells us that following a democratic procedure, an election took place selecting these men as a governing body. They then informed the apostles of the will of the people; after which the apostles, yielding to the people's vote, had a little ceremony inducting these seven into an office before the people.

However, when verse 6 says, they presented these men to the apostles who prayed and laid their hands on them, there was no little religious ceremony. They did not hold an election. There was no inauguration. The Word says the apostles prayed! They first asked prominent leaders to find some help, there were brought seven men to help them; and now the apostles prayed. What did they pray about? I believe they were asking Jesus, the Head of the Church, "Are these the right men, Lord?" If someone brought you seven men from literally thousands, would you not ask the Lord if they were the right men, His choice? It makes perfect sense. They prayed: they did not inaugurate! There was no pomp and circumstance in the early church. They simply inquired of the Lord if these men would do; and it is obvious that the Lord answered, "Yes, they will do."

Had the apostles prayed, and our Lord informed them that these were the wrong men, they would have gone back to square one; but because God's due order took place, and because, as in John 6:29, the people believed in the ones God had sent to lead them, then the works of God were manifested.

They first prayed. Secondly they laid their hands on them to set them apart for the work; for they were approved by the Lord. Hands were laid upon them that they might receive the blessing of God in carrying out their task of distributing food in such a way as to bring peace to the flock. There was no election here to find the will of the people; rather there was a timely unfolding of God's will and wisdom through the apostles (ministry gifts).

Verse 7 reads, "So the word of God spread. The number of disciples in Jerusalem increased rapidly, and a large number of priests became obedient to the faith." (NIV) The blessing of verse 7 would not have been possible if the obedience of verse 6 had not been after the due order of God. God's blessing is upon the following of His due order.

Again, I remind you of the prophetic word given in 1987:

"For after this, (the wind that shakes all that can be shaken), my wind shall blow again. Have you not read how my breath blew on the valley of dry bones. So it shall breathe on you. This wind shall come in equal force with the first wind. This wind too shall have a name. It shall be called the KINGDOM OF GOD, it shall bring MY [*church*] GOVERNMENT AND ORDER." *(brackets added)*

If the Holy Ghost is going to blow upon His church and bring His government and order, that tells me something. It tells me that God's government and order is not presently as He desires for it to be. I'm not at all surprised that He has awakened me on many nights to speak this message to my heart.

Democracy in the church or running God's church by the majority vote of men is one of the greatest false traditions ever to attack the church of the Living God. It has led to the splitting of so many wonderful churches, as good people fought determinedly to have things their own way, rather than submitting to the one God placed in authority, and enjoying the safety and strength of unity. When that error has been corrected, then a tremendous wave of the Spirit in supernatural power is going to move into the church. The works of God will come when we have trusted in God's due order, and received those He has sent. When Jesus was asked, "What shall we do that we might work the works of God?", He responded, " . . . believe on him whom He (God) hath sent." (John 6:28,29) We know this refers first and foremost to Jesus; but I see by the Spirit how that scripture also describes God's desire for His people to view the leadership He gives today in His church as well. God says that if we will receive our ministry gifts whom He has sent, then the supernatural works of God will occur. Because the early church did this, we can read in Acts 6:7, "So the word of God spread. The number of disciples in Jerusalem increased rapidly, and a large number of priests became obedient to the faith." (NIV)

What that verse says to me is that after we have received the revelation of God's due order, rapid growth will come. After God has established His government, it is explosion time. After his people have said, "I yield to the government of God"; then God says, "Multitudes will come in, and rapid growth will occur." We shall do the works of God, and the supernatural shall spring forth upon us as never before.

The latter part of verse 7 is exciting: " . . . a large number of priests became obedient to the faith." The Lord revealed to me how that verse has great relevance for this last day revival, which is coming on the heels of God establishing His government. Those priests were heavily schooled in the meaning and implementation of the theocracy. They totally understood mentally and intellectually the concept of God ruling His people through His man. Some of those priests were very hungry for God, and desirous of serving Him. I believe they were tired of the sham and the emptiness of their religion, which had a form of Godliness but no power at all. They were seeking truth; and when they began to see the supernatural move of God, it reminded them of what they had heard and studied about this God of the Old Testament that for which their hearts had burned. They saw that what was before their eyes was indeed the work of Jehovah God, moving through delegated authority, as He had in olden days. They were thrilled to join the ranks of the believers. Because they were students of the Word and understood the theocracy, they recognized that it was God. They became willing Christians, and a multitude of priests became believers.

The second thing that God spoke to me was that verse 7 is prophetic of our day. As God truly does establish His due order, pastors from other churches, who have preached democracy but secretly hated it, will join the ranks of the churches they have despised, and against which they have preached. The supernatural will begin to be a common thing. The media will pick up on the undeniable things that are about to occur. Pastors from these denominations, who love God with all their hearts, but have been sincerely wrong about the doctrine of the Spirit, will come over and join the ranks of the Spiritually powerful church. Once again a great number of priests/clergy will be obedient to the faith.

Let us do away with the false notions that have clouded the truths of Acts 6 for years:

1. That this was a time in the history of the infant church in which God was setting up His desired government. This scripture has nothing whatsoever to do with setting up church government; however we can see how smoothly a great problem was solved as the Holy Spirit directed God's apostles in appointing deacons. Deacons are servants, not governors.

2. We can do away with the idea that this was a time of inconsistency in God's governmental procedures a time when God sought to initiate a democratic process into thousands of years of theocracy.

There were no votes cast; but, as is consistent with theocracy, those who were appointed by God Himself as gifts in His church did three things: (1) They sought the Lord, (2) They heard His voice, (3) They informed the good people of God, who readily accepted the Word of the Lord from His ministry gifts who were indeed already the government of the church. What happened then? Miracles began in the lives of those who operated joyfully without rebellion to God's due order. Verse 8 reads, "And Stephen, full of faith and power, did great miracles among the people."

Because Stephen, as a servant or deacon, yielded to God's due order, the supernatural began to flow in his life. You can mark this down as well: in this last day, as God is moving to establish the theocracy in the hearts of His people in modern times, those men who fight against theocracy in the church will be hard-pressed to get the supernatural power of God to work in their circumstances of life. Why? Theocracy is God's authority plan. Men who will not submit to God's authority in the church will not be catered to by the power that is at God's disposal. Men who deny God's authority in the ministry gifts He gives will have no authority [power] activated for the needs of their lives. No man can have authority who refuses to operate under authority.

We would do well to say, "Oh God, I yield to your due order right now. I thank You that as I give way to You and Your government, Your power will be available as I need deliverance in this life." Great are the blessings of God coming to those whose hearts are in line with Him and with His delegated authority.

I ran across a scripture in the Weust translation of the New Testament that astounded me when I saw it. Matthew 13:57 in the Weust Expanded Translation reads,

> "And they saw in Him that of which they DISAP-
> PROVED and that which hindered them from ac-
> knowledging His authority, but Jesus said unto them:
> 'A prophet is not without a correct evaluation of his
> worth with a corresponding deference and respect
> which is his due, except in his own country and in his
> own house, and he did not perform there many mir-
> acles, because of their unbelief.'"

Two questions arise: (1) What was it they were not believing? Answer: His authority! He was the One sent to them by God, and they did not believe Him. The result was a lack of the supernatural. (2) Why did they not receive it? Answer: Because they saw in Him that of which they disapproved. They saw in Jesus something they did not like. In Jesus? Yes, they saw in Him something of which they disapproved. That certainly should make pastors the world over feel better.

> "And they saw in Him that of which they disap-
> proved and that which hindered them from acknowl-
> edging His authority . . . ."

Dear saints of God, you can see in any man that of which you do not approve. You can see things which keep you from accepting his authority under God; but God does not find that excusable. Rather He commands:

> "Obey them that have the rule over you, and submit
> yourselves: for they watch for your souls, as they that
> must give account, that they may do it with joy, and not
> with grief: for that is unprofitable for you." (Heb.
> 13:17)

Those who disapprove of and will not obey the leader God has given to them, will lose the supernatural power of God for their lives.

The one crucial fact in this particular area of understanding, is that you must always separate the man, with his human weaknesses, from the position of authority in which God has chosen to place him. God does; and if you don't, you will find yourself fighting against God.

I realize I am not the shepherd of a flock because I am so good. Why then? Because God Almighty brought me to this place and said, "I'm giving you to these people. This is My will for you." The word of the Lord came unto me as I sought His direction in Georgia. Haggai 1:8 instantly became *rhema* (God's spoken Word) to me:

> "Go up to the mountain (Sioux City for me) and
> bring wood, and build the house: and I will take
> pleasure in it, and I will be glorified, saith the Lord."

God sends true pastors to His people. We must separate the man from the position, for failing to do so is very detrimental to our own good.

To my shame, I can attest to this truth through my own experience. Years ago I found myself criticizing a man of God who was commonly known for his aggravating personality. He spoke at a meeting I was attending, and his ways of communication were, to me, very caustic. I sensed no love in his delivery and was irritated to see him on the platform. I opened my mouth and expressed my disdain in several ways.

The Holy Spirit spoke in an undeniable fashion within me, saying something I shall never forget. He said, "Those statements will shorten your life unless you repent."

I repented immediately, and have never forgotten the moment I learned never to speak against any servant of God. Paul chastened the Roman Christians for doing this by asking:

> "Who art thou that judgest another man's servant?
> to his own master he standeth or falleth. Yea, he shall
> be holden up: for God is able to make him stand."
> Romans 14:4

Because I desire the supernatural God of Heaven to find pleasure in me, and I also desire His power to operate freely in the affairs of my life, I have determined to submit myself to the authority of God and those He has placed above me.

You may wonder, "Who is above you, as a senior pastor?"

(1) God is certainly above me as His ministry gift and as the God of Heaven and Creator of all things. Why people believe they can better control the man of God democratically than the God of Heaven can control him theocratically is beyond me.

(2) God has given me a wonderful pastor to whom I submit for instruction and correction. He is in authority over me because God has put us together in that relationship. Along with my pastor, other great men of God have been made accessible to me by the Lord of the church for counselling and encouragement.

(3) My dear mate and helpmeet in the gospel constantly watches me with vigilant love to keep me right in my thinking and approach to the ministry.

(4) The other pastors of this congregation are highly esteemed in my sight and I can submit to them, receiving their loving counsel as well.

If we will only follow God's plan, flowing freely under His delegated authority, great and mighty wonders will be wrought in Jesus' name!

When God Relinquishes Control

CHAPTER

6

Consider with me again the account given in Acts 6:1-7:

"In those days when the number of disciples was increasing, the Grecian Jews among them complained against the Hebraic Jews because their widows were being overlooked in the daily distribution of food. So the twelve gathered all the disciples together and said, 'It would not be right for us to neglect the ministry of the word of God in order to wait on tables. Brothers, choose seven men from among you who are known to be full of the Spirit and wisdom. We will turn this responsibility over to them and we will give our attention to prayer and the ministry of the word.' This proposal pleased the whole group. They chose Stephen, a man full of faith and of the Holy Spirit; also Philip, Prochorus, Nicanor, Timon, Parmenas, and Nicholas from Antioch, a convert to Judaism. They presented these men to the apostles, who prayed and laid their hands on them. So the word of God spread. The number of disciples in Jerusalem increased rapidly, and a large number of priests became obedient to the faith." (NIV)

In our democratic national government, which we support and love with all of our hearts, we are satiated with democratic thought forms. It is extremely difficult for some to make that transition out of the nation and into the church. The church is not a democracy. The church operates so very differently. To carry democracy into the church is to insure two things: death and failure to the church.

At first glance, we might assume that some of the large, well organized denominational churches are very blessed; but let's look more closely. Can we find deliverance for those oppressed by devils there? Can we find healing for cancer there? Can we learn something of God other than the new birth there; if indeed the new birth is even taught? Soon we must conclude that the democratic church has failed to demonstrate the power of the gospel.

I have had several years of experience myself in a failing, democratic form of man-ruled church. I was an "up and coming" young minister in a church like that and spent twenty-five years there. I have seen first hand the tragedy that can come when democracy is practiced in God's church. The norm for those churches, with a few wonderful exceptions, was tragedy and failure. God had very little to do with the government of the church; and He had nothing to do with the selection of the pastor. Actually they did not have pastors: they had, and have, "preachers". There is a great difference! The preachers were elected by men. Sometimes the whole church voted on who the preacher was going to be. The result of democracy in the churches I know of personally, was that many of the board members, who in these churches were called elders (overseers, pastors), were adulterers, tax evaders, alcoholics. All manner of severe problems attached themselves to many of the men making up the church government. Although there were a few fine spiritual individuals blended into the church governments, the church never could seem to get off the ground. The few spiritual men were of precious little good in the overall necessity for spiritual leadership. Regardless of how much teaching was done on the qualifications of elders and deacons, the result was always the same. Sadly, their perception of what elders and deacons were, was false; for to put the responsibility of the government of the church upon the sheep, rather than the pastor (true elder or overseer), was never the intention of God.

Every time men begin to vote in the church, God relinquishes control. When God relinquishes control, He gives it over into the control of men. Once men have control, it is down hill from there.

God spoke to me early one morning and said, no doubt with tongue in cheek, "There was one time I told men to vote." I said, "When was that Lord?" He said, "It was when Moses had come down off the mountain and found the people worshipping the golden calf." They were worshipping the calf by majority rule. They all decided to sin; and Moses replied in this manner, "You want a choice? OK, I'll give you a choice. Choose! Are you with God and me, or are you with this idol and the devil?" Those that chose God and Moses went to one side and those who chose sin went to the other. God then told Moses to instruct the Levites to take their swords and slay all who had voted against God. The next day a plague fell on the rest of them, and they died by the thousands. Thus we read of one more result of the majority vote in the church in the wilderness.

When it comes to God and His church, those who choose democracy choose destruction in one form or another. If you choose democracy in the church, eventually Satan will "have you for lunch". I personally know a man who, after having been taught on God's theocratic plan for church government, left the church, taking those he could persuade to follow, and established a democratic church with himself as the pastor. Within a few short months, the congregation had voted him out! The next pastor they voted in only lasted a few weeks; and finally the group gasped its last democratic breath and died. This would be funny if it were not for the wounded and disillusioned lives left in the wake of a man doing what seemed right in his own eyes. I want God's best; and the way to attain God's best is to go God's way and not man's way.

Let's take a further look at the term, *deacon*. The Greek word is *diakonos*, which describes the "servant, or one who serves in menial matters". The adjective "menial" is not a derogatory description. The importance of service in menial matters is beyond words. We could not take care of spiritual things, were it not for the service of the ushers, the parking attendants, the janitors, the kitchen helpers, the secretarial staff, the grounds people and on and on. There is a great service to the Lord to be performed by all such wonderful and needed helpers in the church. However, we must see that the whole purpose for those original seven such individuals, was to take the burden of those "menial matters" from the shoulders of those church leaders (ministry gifts), enabling them to do the work of the Spirit in giving themselves to prayer and ministry of the Word.

The deacon was in no way part of the government of the church. He assisted the ministry gift as needed and required. Strongs Dictionary, probably the most distinguished of all Bible reference sources, defines the word, number 1248, *Diakonia*, "attender as a servant", or *eleemosynary*, which means "unpaid aid". So we see that as the ministry gift is in full-time service to the Lord and generally makes his living in this way; the deacon, on the other hand, is unsalaried by the church, but serves the Lord in most cases while doing something else for a living. The next word, number 1249, is *Diako*, meaning "one who runs errands, an attendant, a waiter at a table, or other menial duties, technically used of deacons or deaconesses."

The word *deacon* also refers generally to the work of the pastor, in that he serves food (God's Word) to the sheep (God's people); and he is a servant of God. However, the pastor is a servant under the authority of the Lord, and not under the authority of the people. The deacon is a servant to the ministry gift, and serves God by serving God's man.

I was raised in a church that is democratic in nature. What they term "elders" and "deacons" ruled the church and assumed authority over the minister or preacher. He was not a pastor or overseer, but a minister and servant under the authority of the people. In all reality, he is a deacon serving the "board of elders and deacons". It is my belief that such a concept is in exact opposition to Biblical teaching, yet it is practiced in many denominations on a worldwide scale. The preacher was in bondage to the church board and was viewed as a hireling. He therefore did not stay long. The result was and is that every two to five years the people begin to notice in the preacher "that of which they disapprove" (Mt. 13:57), and desire to "vote him out". At the same time, the preacher begins wishing for a new set of problem sheep under which to serve and starts "church hunting". The church is totally run by the will of the people. God is, in a manner of speaking, at the mercy of the denominational box into which those folks have placed themselves. The decisions of the church are made, for the most part, by the thinking of the people. God has very little to do with it.

Please understand it is not my intent to belittle the good that is done in these churches. Many people are brought to a saving knowledge of Jesus, for which I praise God! However, the new babes often never grow beyond that point. They are left bereft of power to succeed, for the teaching stops there. That is not to say that they do not go to heaven, for most assuredly they do. However, since the supernatural has been confined to ages past in that church, there are few miracles there to speak about, other than the greatest miracle of salvation from sin. I am not making light at all of the wonderful salvation which I, and multitudes of others, found there. I would, however, point out that in the majority of democratically run churches, the miracle working power of God Almighty has been done away with in the theological teaching of the church. Therefore, no faith exists for their manifestation.

The Lord will only be able to operate minimally in that type situation; but great is the grace and mercy of the Lord. Because of His lovingkindness, He will operate anywhere He can, to the degree that He can. He loves people and desires to help them. However, His word is clear regarding the government of the church. He desires theocracy. He desires to deal with people from His throne, through the leadership of ministry gifts whom He appoints, anoints, and sets in position as He wills.

Genesis 6:9 reads, "This is the account of Noah. Noah was a righteous man, blameless among the people of his time, and he walked with God." Verse 13, "So God said to Noah, I am going to put an end to all the people, for the earth is filled with violence because of them. I am surely going to destroy both them and the earth." (NIV)

So we see that from the beginning God has dealt with the earth through one individual, His man. II Peter 2:5 says that God saved Noah, who was a "preacher of righteousness".

When God was ready to do a tremendous thing of great importance upon the earth, He formed no committees and elected no boards; rather He worked through His man. He dealt with one man. It has been so from the beginning. God is a God Who deals with order: not the order of men, but His own order. More than one head constitutes "too many chiefs and not enough Indians". I believe the scripture makes it very clear that God desires to deal with one man, His man, in the accomplishing of the leadership of the church. During the Old Testament age, He dealt through His man the Prophet, until men rebelled against that plan. In the New Testament, and particularly in the end of the world, He is once more establishing His theocratic government with His ministry gifts. Apostles, prophets, evangelists, pastors and teachers are to be the government of the New Testament Church. Any other form of government in the church cannot obtain the best of God. Other forms may obtain some of God's blessings; but I, for one, want His best.

God never intended that Israel should be governed by a king. God is the King of Kings; and He desired to rule Israel Himself through His prophet. He, however, realizing the wickedness and stubbornness of that nation, prophesied as early as Deuteronomy that one day Israel would turn their back on theocracy and demand a king. We read in Deuteronomy 17:14:

> "When you enter the land the Lord your God is giving you and have taken possession of it and settled in it, and you say, 'Let us set a king over us like all the nations around us . . .'" (NIV)

God prophesied that His people would begin to want a man-ruled form of government years and years before the time they would ask for a king. It is always very sad when the people of God care more about peer pressure than God pressure.

Why would the people of God ever presume that an earthly king would be superior to God's leadership? Why would the King of Kings desire a mere man as king over His people? However, that was the will of the majority; and it brought them much grief. Centuries have passed; still, God is King, and I believe He still desires to govern the church today through His ministry gifts.

The scripture describes what a sad day it was when they asked God for a king. I Samuel 8:4-9 reads:

> "So all the elders of Israel gathered together and came to Samuel at Ramah. They said to him, 'You are old, and your sons do not walk in your ways; now appoint a king to lead us, such as all the other nations have.' But when they said, 'Give us a king to lead us,' this displeased Samuel; so he prayed to the Lord. And the Lord told him: 'Listen to all that the people are saying to you; it is not you they have rejected, but they have rejected me as their king. As they have done from the day I brought them out of Egypt until this day, forsaking me and serving other Gods, so they are doing to you. Now listen to them; but warn them solemnly and let them know what the king who will reign over them will do.'" NIV

That day, Israel lost the greatest King that any man could have, the

Living God. Notice the Lord said, "It is not you they have rejected, but . . . me." (verse 7) I believe the Lord is saying to us today in the church of the Living God, that when people demand the democratic right to cast a vote based on their opinions in crucial church matters, they are rejecting God now as Israel did then. Israel went on with their traditional worship, but they lost God as their king. We may go on with our man ruled churches, but for the most part, we have lost the presence and mighty power of God in our churches.

The people of Israel groaned and complained under the burdens which they brought on themselves by rejecting God's leadership. So today, some of God's people need to wake up! They insist on democracy in the church and wonder why things don't go well for them. They can grow to a certain stage in God and then can go no further. The degree to which men submit themselves to the true government of God, is the degree to which they grow in Him. There may seem to be some exceptions to that rule, but I believe the exceptions are very few.

The sad truth is that many saints are appalled at the idea of God leading the church through one man, for a variety of reasons, such as: "We were just not brought up that way", "We never did things that way in our church", "I don't buy this theocratic stuff; the pastor just wants to be a dictator", "I don't trust the pastor to lead, we must keep the pastor under control through an elected board." Those precious, tradition-bound saints will never get above where they are right now in their Christian walk, for we are living in the end of the world; and God has said that He will establish His government in the church.

Remember the Lord's words to Samuel, "It is not you they have rejected, but . . . me." (I Sam. 8:7) Take inventory, saints of God. If our choice of church government constitutes a rejection of God, is it worth it? You can love God with all your heart and still reject Him. How? Simply by not doing what He says.

There are many wonderful people who would never consider themselves to be rebels; and yet any man or woman who takes their own way, rather than the way God has set forth in His Word, is in rebellion. Loving God and loving the pastor is not necessarily enough we must still obey the Word. Jesus said, "If you love Me, keep My commandments." (John 14:15)

God desired to use His prophet then, and God has never changed His mind. God never has to change His mind, because all His ways are perfect. He's never thought of a bad plan. The only reason God has had to prepare a new plan is because His people rebelled against Him. He started the church in the wilderness with Pastor Moses, and soon added 70 associate pastors. Moses was a prophet of God and a type or fore shadow of God's New Testament leadership. Today God desires to govern the church via His ministry gifts, who correspond with the ministry of the Old Testament prophet. God does not desire to govern the church with deacons, nor by elders, as the term is defined in many churches today.

Scripturally speaking, what are true "elders"? This is another very misunderstood term in the Word of God. Vine's Expository Dictionary says, the term *presbuteros* is the word we translate as "elders". His definition reads: "In the Christian churches, those who, being raised up and qualified by the work of the Holy Spirit, were appointed to have the spiritual care of, and to exercise oversight over, the churches. To these, the term bishops, *episcopi*, or overseers, is applied. The latter term (*episcopoi*) indicating the nature of their work, (*presyteria*) the maturity of spiritual experience." (An Expository Dictionary of New Testament Words, W. E. Vine, p. 21)

Elders are *pastors* "persons raised up and qualified by the work of the Holy Spirit, appointed to have the spiritual care of, and to exercise oversight over the churches". Our definition must be God's definition rather than man's if we desire to be correct. He honors His word above His name. If we want to be blessed, we must do things God's way. Elders are ministry gifts as listed in Ephesians 4:11-13:

> "And he gave some, apostles; and some, prophets; and some, evangelists; and some, pastors and teachers; For the perfecting of the saints, for the work of the ministry, for the edifying of the body of Christ: Till we all come in the unity of the faith, and of the knowledge of the Son of God, unto a perfect man, unto the measure of the stature of the fulness of Christ . . . ."

Apostles, prophets, evangelists, pastors and teachers are to be the "elders" as defined above! Men who are not ministry gifts given by Jesus to the church are not scriptural "elders". We believe in a plurality of elders (or pastors) in the church. The number of elders in a particular congregation is dependant on how many the church is able to support at its present size. If the church is small and has only one true pastor, then the church has only one "elder". If the church is only large enough to support one elder/pastor, then there can be no plurality of elders until the people, having submitted themselves to God and their pastor, bring forth fruit and growth enough to add more overseers for their spiritual care. The absolute worst thing that can be done, is to be shackled by the false teaching on eldership which would bring unqualified people in to have oversight and spiritual care of God's people.

There can only be a plurality of elders as God gives them into a situation. Elders are ministry gifts given by God, not voted in by the will of the people. The one term we generally use for these ministry gifts is "pastor" in the local church. While it is wonderful to have a strong team of elders/pastors, still there must always be the senior or head pastor, who is ultimately responsible before God.

Some have been confused, thinking that an "elder" must always mean someone older in years. There is more than one word translated "elder" in the Bible. One of them, of course, does mean simply an "older man". However, that is not the word for "elder" which is used in reference to church government. The word *presbus* is used to describe an older man. *Presbus* does not mean "pastor", but simply men older in years. Acts 2:17 says, "… your old men will dream dreams." simply referring to older men chronologically.

Age has nothing to do with maturity in the Lord. David was just a child when he slew Goliath, and he went on to become the greatest king in history. Jeremiah was a very young man when God called him to serve, and cried out, "Ah, Lord God! behold, I cannot speak: for I am a child!" (Jer. 1:6) Many younger men and women are far more mature in the things of God than their elders in years. In the theocracy, God calls whomever He will, and at what ever age He wills, to be in positions of authority in His kingdom. Therefore, when referring to church government, an "elder" is synonymous with the terms "pastor", "bishop", "overseer" or "shepherd"; and this calling may be applied to those of God's choosing, no matter their age. The wise and spiritually discerning man will place himself under that authority.

An elder is a ministry gift. Now there are elders or ministry gifts given to the local church; and there are elders or ministry gifts given by God to the church at large. In the local church, the senior pastor is the man immediately under God (also receiving guidance and counsel from the pastor God gives to him), and all other ministry gifts are under his authority. Those whom we refer to as associate pastors, are under the authority of the senior pastor in the local church.

Now let's deal with a very important question. In a theocracy, should the pastor die or go into sin of an irreparable nature, what are the sheep to do?

Sheep do not go shepherd hunting! Can you imagine a bunch of sheep going out on the hillside looking for someone to choose as their shepherd? That is not God's plan. Should the local pastor be taken out of the ministry, for any reason, then the elders, or ministry gifts at large, come into the local situation to help find the answer for the flock.

Throughout the New Testament we find time after time where Paul, the ministry gift of apostle called not just to one local body of believers, but to God's church all over the world, would deliver instructions to the various local churches as needed. He boldly used God's authority to oust those leaders who were causing division and offenses "by good words and fair speeches deceiving the hearts of the simple". (Rom. 16:17) He pronounced a curse on those who were perverting the Gospel of Christ, troubling the Galatians. (Gal. 1:7) He "delivered unto Satan" Hymenaeus and Alexander, who began with pure faith, but "made shipwreck". (I Tim. 1:19,20) Conversely, he specifically instructed the churches on who to follow as leaders, commending those who were one heart and one spirit with him in the Lord, commanding the churches to receive them. [Examples: Marcus to the church at Colosse (Col. 4:10); Phoebe to the church at Rome (Rom. 16:1,2)]

Every pastor needs a pastor; someone to whom he may turn. If you are reading this work as a senior pastor, or as a ministry gift given to the church at large, and you have no one under whose authority you submit yourself, I encourage you to let God meet that need in your life.

How often we tell people who think they don't need to be part of a local church that there are no "lone rangers" in God's family. The same is true for all ministry gifts: we must let God keep us properly positioned in His chain of command. In whatever position the Lord of the Church chooses to give us in His army, our Great Commander has made provision not only for His heavenly covering, but also for the earthly covering of His church. Every apostle, prophet, evangelist, pastor, teacher and saint must submit himself to those of like anointing and to those over him in the Lord. Remember Peter's words in I Peter 5:5:

> " . . . Yea, all [of you] be subject one to another, and
> be clothed with humility: for God resisteth the proud,
> and giveth grace to the humble."

What a blessed safety there is in God's plan of order!

God has given me a wonderful pastor to whom I submit for instruction and correction. He is in authority over me because God has put us together in that relationship. Should things go wrong in the church I lead, he would come in and work with the associate pastors of this church to set things in order. A theocracy is always supplied by God and not by men. There is great security in the theocracy.

God never intended that should the shepherd (pastor, elder) of the sheep go wrong, the sheep should have an election in order to find a new shepherd. Countless wonderful churches have been split down through the years as the sheep squabbled and fought over the shepherd they liked best! God has provided a plan theocratically, through delegated authority, and through the ministry gifts given to the world-wide church, for such problems to be handled.

I Samuel 1:3 reads, "And the two sons of Eli, Hophni and Phineas, the priests of the Lord, were there (in Shiloh)." Now these two were rotten to the core. Talk about rotten pastors! I Samuel 2:12 says, "Eli's sons were wicked men. They had no regard for the Lord." (NIV)

From the beginning of time there have been two major sin snares of the devil, set to entrap God's men. They are (1) the misuse of money and (2) sexual sins. I Samuel 2:17 says of these two:

"This sin of the young men was very great in the Lord's sight, for they were treating the Lord's offering with contempt." (NIV)

Of course, we would relate to that "offering" in terms of possessions or money. Then verse 22 reveals the sexual sins:

"Now Eli, who was very old, heard about everything his sons were doing to all Israel and how they slept with the women who served at the entrance of the Tent of Meeting." (NIV)

This story reminds us of the CBS evening news! However, God did not panic when Eli's sons went bad. He didn't just quit everything, saying, "My choice of leadership went wrong; My plan failed, so I'd better just let men decide how to run things themselves." If we keep on reading we will find that the people still brought the offerings to God's priests. The women still came to worship God and to work in the tent of meeting.

When the sin of the first major TV evangelist went out across America in 1987, certain people came to me warning me to disclose every minute detail of the ministry, or trouble was on the way. We may surely learn from the mistakes of others; however the Holy Spirit never uses fear tactics to motivate God's leaders. Men of God down through history have fallen into sin. That is no reason to panic. I assure you the plan of God will go on. Satan would like for the church to panic and bolt one way or the other. Those that bolt will find themselves in more danger by far, than those who consistently, without fear, keep on walking in the peace of God, being fruitful as they go.

God doesn't panic when His creation falls: He just keeps on being God. For every one who falls, there are thousands of good men of God out there who are holding steady and walking out God's plans. For the one who falls and repents, there is God's great love, mercy and forgiveness.

When Eli's sons became corrupt, God did not quit receiving offerings by His priests; nor did He tell all the ladies they had better stay home from church because these two guys had a problem with money and sex. God did not change His method of operation, and has not to this very day. God knows how to deal with His servants who go the wrong way.

Eli said to his sinful boys in I Samuel 2:25:

> "If a man sins against another man, God may mediate for him; but if a man sins against the Lord, who will intercede for him?' His sons however did not listen to their fathers rebuke. . . ." (NIV)

So there we see the problem; and the answer to that problem lies in the very next verse. God always has the answer; no one needs to panic. The next verse reads:

> "And the boy Samuel continued to grow in stature and in favor with the Lord and with men."(I Sam. 2:26)

Samuel was God's answer. The problem was bad pastors; and the answer was that God had a great pastor waiting in the wings.

In I Samuel 2:34-35, God said to Eli:

> "And what happens to your two sons, Hophni and Phineas, will be a sign to you they will both die on the same day. I will raise up for myself a faithful priest, who will do according to what is in my heart and mind. I will firmly establish his house, and he will minister before my anointed one always."

Then we read of God's faithfulness to perform His Word in chapter 3:10:

> "The Lord came and stood there, calling as at the other times, 'Samuel! Samuel!' Then Samuel said, 'Speak, for your servant is listening.'" (NIV)

There was God's answer. It was simple, wasn't it? There was nothing to panic about. Israel's pastors were bad. God took care of it, but not through an election, not through a pulpit committee, or a board of what men call elders and deacons. He simply opened His mouth and called to the one He had standing in the wings. God always has a plan! We get nervous because we don't always know His plan. God said, "I WILL RAISE UP FOR MYSELF A FAITHFUL PRIEST," (a pastor, ministry gift, leader or overseer). God said He would raise up one for Himself!

Today as we follow God's due order, should the pastor fall, God is still well able to raise up for Himself, another. He will do so by following after the due order. He will do so through delegated authority, through His theocracy using His ministry gift set in place over that local pastor, to set things in order.

Democratically run churches have no other recourse but trial and error, electing men that happen to tickle the fancy of the majority. God's way is good and simple; and brings great security to the flock.

What about those churches who do not operate under any authority but their own? Those churches where the one who is to feed and care for God's flock is hired and fired by a board of elected officials? They simply have to go about things in the same old hit and miss fashion, as has happened for years. Maybe they will find and vote in God's man, and maybe they will get the choice of the flesh.

Every pastor needs a pastor. Every church needs to have a relation-ship with others of like faith, to whom they can go for delegated and theocratic assistance, in such times as we have discussed. No church should be in bondage to an organization; however, every congrega-tion should have men of God on a higher level than themselves, to render assistance as needed.

God is well able to run His church. He always has a plan; and His plan always works!

In One Accord

CHAPTER

In the last chapter of this book, we will look at the all important subject of being of one mind, one accord and one heart with the Lord, and with His delegated authority. In the 20th chapter of John we find a powerful example of oneness in Jesus and His faithful chosen followers. John 20:21,22 reads:

> "Then said Jesus to them again, Peace be unto you: as my Father has sent me, even so send I you. And when He had said this, He breathed on them, and saith unto them, Receive ye the Holy Ghost . . . "

In that moment, He breathed His Spirit into them, and they became one with Him. Instantly they were not only born again, but they began to be infused with His understanding, direction and purpose. Upon receiving the Holy Spirit from the Lord, these men were enabled to come into a true unity with Jesus, the One Whom God had sent to lead them. Up until this moment they had been filled with fear and confusion as they had watched Jesus suffer and die. However, now by His wonderful Spirit, they could receive understanding of the purpose and plan of God for redemption through Jesus; and with unified hearts they could go forth in His Name, fulfilling their own callings. Through the Spirit which Jesus imparted they were enabled to pass along the glorious gospel - the vision or purpose of Jesus their Leader - to those they were now called to lead. Therefore we read in Acts 1:14, "These all continued with one accord in prayer and supplication, with the women, and Mary the mother of Jesus . . . ", and in Acts 2:1, "And when the day of Pentecost was fully come, they were all in one accord in one place."

Why? What brought about this oneness, that so characterized these disciples? The answer is that they had received the Spirit of Jesus their Leader; and the Holy Spirit is the One Who enables us to walk together in unity under the direction of God's leaders. He had said to them, "Peace I give to you." He was the Prince of Peace; therefore, having received His Spirit of Peace, they were in one accord. The receiving of Jesus' Spirit into them was the enabling factor that brought about the fulfillment of Jesus' prayer for them in John 17:11:

>"And now I am no more in the world, but these are
>in the world, and I come to thee. Holy Father, keep
>through thine own name those whom thou hast given
>me, that they may be one, as we are."

In fact, in the same chapter and verse 21, Jesus prayed the very same prayer for oneness concerning you and me:

>"That they may all be one; as thou, Father, art in me,
>and I in thee, that they also may be one in us: that the
>world may believe that thou hast sent me."

Unity is impossible without a heart determination to be in one accord with God's leaders. God's local churches can only be fully effective when His people purpose in their hearts to "endeavor to keep the unity of the Spirit" (Eph. 4:3) by having the same vision as the pastors whom they follow and the desire to work in harmony and peace with their fellow workers. The Amplified Bible's version of this passage reads:

>"Be eager and strive earnestly to guard and keep the
>harmony and oneness produced by the Spirit in the
>binding power of peace."

Unity would be impossible among a people who are unique in their thought processes, diversified in their backgrounds and varied in their levels of understanding without the Holy Spirit, Who enables us to flow with God's chain of command. He provides the power to be one under His chosen leader: our job is to be obedient while earnestly guarding and keeping our unity. It is extremely important to note that when we use the terminology, "in one accord", we are in fact referring to the oneness of thought and singleness of direction that can only occur by the Holy Spirit, so that all are thinking, moving and striving in unity toward the same goal. Great victory is assured as we allow the Holy Spirit to bring us into one accord with each other and the leadership. In the beginning of the church it was so, and it is so today. Oneness demands a unified heart. The sheep must be in one accord with the shepherd; the soldiers must be in one accord with the general; and the disciples must be in one accord - that is operating with the same understanding - with the teacher. Being in one accord is of prime importance to the success of any group.

Timothy operated under the anointing of Paul's ministry. He became one with Paul in the understanding and implementation of the vision for ministry which God had placed in the Apostle Paul. The associate pastors of any church must operate under the influence of the senior pastor. His heart's desires, given by God, must be transferred to them in order for oneness, unity, and victory to ensue. We see the immense success that came to the first apostles of our Lord. They affected the whole world for Jesus by receiving His Spirit and coming into a place of one accord.

The necessity of being in one accord is by no means a new concept, for it has been shown to us throughout the Holy Word. Moses was being worn out by reason of all the counseling and judging necessary to keep order among the thousands of Israelites who had left Egypt. Jethro, his father-in-law, had suggested that he appoint judges over the people. Moses did so, and the Word tells us that God put the spirit of Moses on all the elders of Israel, making them one with Moses. So the understanding and thought processes of Moses were somehow transferred to these elders of Israel who handled things for God and Moses. They were in one accord with Moses. The record of this incident dates back almost to the beginning of things. Numbers 11:17 reads:

> " . . . and I will take of the spirit which is upon thee, and will put it upon them; and they shall bear the burden of the people with thee, that thou bear it not thyself alone." We also read in verse 25: "And the Lord came down in a cloud, and spake unto him, and took of the spirit that was upon him, and gave it unto the seventy elders: and it came to pass, that, when the spirit rested upon them, they prophesied, and did not cease."

The same spirit of direction and understanding that was upon

Moses, was imparted to those in leadership under him. God knew then, and knows now, how important it is that those in leadership be of the same spirit . . . IN ONE ACCORD. His desire is always to take the vision and direction He has planted in His leader and place it upon those serving under him - making them one; for so it is in God's theocracy. Should He take the spirit of the majority of those serving in helping positions, and place it upon the leader, theocracy has fallen and democracy rules. The leader is then a puppet of the masses and is really no leader at all. God wants His leaders free to hear and follow His voice alone, free to be "God-pleasers" rather than "men-pleasers".

The great weapon of oneness in heart and soul must be realized in the outworkings of every church that is striving toward any goal for God in this world. If men and women are united in the Spirit of God, and are one in heart and mind with the man whom God has placed in authority, success will come!

We see this illustrated in the astonishing relationship of David and Jonathan. I Samuel 18:1 reads:

> "And it came to pass, when he had made an end of
> speaking unto Saul, that the soul of Jonathan was knit
> with the soul of David, and Jonathan loved him as his
> own soul."

We see here that God had put the soul [we could safely say the understanding and direction] of David upon Jonathan, Saul's own son. For in truth, David was the man chosen by God to sit in the place of authority in Israel under God. Saul was the choice of the people, and not the choice of God. In order for the plans of God to come to fruition, He left Saul in his haughty, rebellious state and began to deal with David and Jonathan. Knowing the necessity of imparting direction and understanding from the true leader to those in other leadership positions, God took of David's soul and knit it together with Jonathan's.

It was more important that Jonathan and David be one, than that Jonathan support his father, a demoniac and an illegitimate leader chosen by the will of the people.

Oh, how important this is for our churches today! The associate pastors must be one in heart and mind with the senior pastor, and the congregation must flow in obedience and love under those whom they have been called to serve. The accusing and fault finding person will always cry out against the man of God's choice: this has been Satan's method of blocking the moving of God among His people from the beginnings of time. However, in these last days it is vital that the people of God understand authority, and with faithful hearts and supporting words, serve in their positions in order that Jesus' prayer for our unity might be realized, and the Bride prepared for His return.

Proverbs 13:20 says, "He who walks with wise men will be wise." We then can assume that by extension "He who walks with angry men will be angry. He who walks with striving men will be striving." It will work in the negative just as it works in the positive. But those of a pure heart will refuse to speak ill of God's anointed. Saul spoke of David to Jonathan in I Samuel 20:31,32:

> "For as long as the son of Jesse liveth upon the ground, thou shalt not be established, nor thy kingdom. Wherefore now send and fetch him unto me, for he shall surely die. And Jonathan answered Saul his father, and said unto him, Wherefore shall he be slain? What hath he done?"

Because David and Jonathan were of one accord and one heart, Jonathan refused to allow even the king to make critical statements regarding David. Jonathan protected David even to the point of jeopardizing his own life. We read in the very next verse, "And Saul cast a javelin at him to smite him . . . ." (I Sam. 20:33)

Though it may not be the popular course, God looks with favor upon those who protect His anointed ones. More than once I have warned those who lightly accused and criticized the servants of God. We see the end of Saul, the enemy of David and God. We see the horrible life lived by Saul and the terrible things he suffered. He thought he was God's man, and all the while he was warring against God's true man. Jonathan, on the other hand, had the good sense to recognize the anointing of God and support it. In I Samuel 23:17, Jonathan said to David:

" . . . Fear not: for the hand of Saul my father shall
not find thee; and thou shalt be king over Israel . . . "

There must be a joining of hearts among the servants of the Lord
who serve as the pastors of a church. That same spirit will then file
down through the ranks. Psalm 133:1,2 paints a vivid picture of how
the unity of God's people is to flow from His leader down to touch
each follower:

"Behold, how good and how pleasant it is for brethren to dwell together in unity! It is like the precious
ointment upon the head, that ran down the beard, even
Aaron's beard: that went down to the skirts of his
garments . . . "

The anointing of Aaron as God's ministry gift to the people was a
beautiful type of the anointing work of the Holy Spirit upon those
whom God calls to lead today. Just as the unifying oil ran over the
head, down the beard, and down the skirts covering Aaron's entire
body, so God intends for the vision and purpose He has placed in His
leader to flow to every member of the body of Christ, making them one
in the bonds of love. If the associate pastors and leaders over each area
of ministry in a church are firmly in touch with the heart of the senior
pastor, that oneness will be found in the staff and in the rest of the
flock. When this is true, God is greatly glorified; and the church will
find tremendous victory. Verse 3 of Psalm 133 continues:

" . . . for there (in this place of unity among the brethren) the Lord commanded the blessing, even life for
evermore."

However, if one associate chooses to be in opposition to the pastor,
trouble will begin to erupt here and there; for the vision of the leader
has been refused. Satan will work his hardest to cause that kind of
thing to happen, for it gives him an open door for "confusion and every
evil work" in God's precious church. (See James 3:16) That associate

places himself in grave danger; for he has put himself at enmity with the Lord of the Church.

The story of Absalom is the perfect example of the pain and destruction that erupts when there is strife among the leadership of God's people. Absalom was a prince in Israel, serving under his father King David, the anointed man of God. Absalom, however, refused to be of one heart with David; instead he began to undercut and usurp the power given by God to David alone. He criticized the way David did things to the people. Through enticing words, he began to steal the hearts of the people away from their God-given leader. People who do that often will find themselves in a very precarious situation after a time. We read of Absalom in II Samuel 18:9 these words:

> " . . . And Absalom rode upon a mule, and the mule
> went under the thick boughs of a great oak, and his
> head caught hold of the oak, and he was taken up
> between the heaven and the earth; and the mule that
> was under went away."

Soon soldiers, who had remained in David's army, found him there and slew him. Thus we see the end of those who become rebellious in their own spirit against the direction of God's chosen leader. We see the tragic end that can come when being in one accord has not occurred between the man God anoints to lead and those under his leadership. David referred to such individuals who were of another mind as "strange children". In Psalm 144:7,8 we read:

> "Send thine hand from above: rid me, and deliver
> me out of great waters, from the hand of strange
> children; Whose mouth speaketh vanity, and their
> right hand is a right hand of falsehood."

This is a perfect description of Absalom, David's own son, who had rebelled against him. In practically every church that has ever existed, out of the family of our great Heavenly Father, "strange children" have emerged. They are men and women who have judged them-selves to be better qualified to run the church than the persons chosen by God. They are people who are of "another mind" - one contrary to the leadership of the ministry. Of such were Hymenaeus and Philetus. Paul said in II Timothy 2:16-18:

> "But shun profane and vain babblings: for they will increase unto more ungodliness. And their word will eat as doth a canker: of whom is Hymenaeus and Philetus; Who concerning the truth have erred, saying that the resurrection is past already; and overthrow the faith of some."

These two men told the people, "Paul is off course. He is not teaching you properly. He wasn't handling things well. Let me tell you how it really should be." They overthrew the faith of some. They were in the family of God, but were "strange children". They were men who refused to be of one accord and of the same understanding and direction with Paul the apostle, who had received the grace for his calling from God. (See Rom. 1:5)

Most people are followers and not leaders. We must endeavor to remember that God, in His great love, has given to the sheep of His pasture, shepherds hand picked by Himself. We must follow the shepherd God has given us. We must also refuse the 10,000 others who would like for us to follow their leading, rather than the leading of our God-given shepherd. I Corinthians 4:15 reads:

> "For though ye have ten thousand instructors in Christ, yet have ye not many father . . . "

The pastor has been given to the church as a "father figure" to protect, guide and encourage those he leads on to maturity. God set it up that way. Ephesians 4:11 tells us that one of the precious gifts God has given to His church is pastors (elders, overseers). For the local church, the pastor is the most important of those gifts. He is the prime-minister of the Lord unto His people. Be very careful of others who would like to impose themselves upon you, be it in Bible studies that are not sanctioned by the church, or fellowship meetings unknown by your pastor. Normally if you look into the history of the people responsible for directing these meetings, you will find they have been involved in trouble in every church they have attended. Be careful! For though it be ever so gently and subtly, they would impose their divisive hearts upon you, planting seeds of criticism and bitterness against the one God has sent to lead you safely onward to victory. Red flags should go up in your spirit instantly when you first hear the words, "We don't agree with the pastor." Watch out! Satan is still around to provide modern day Absaloms, Hymenaeus's or Philetus's, "whose mouth speaketh vanity, and their right hand is a right hand of falsehood." (Ps. 144:8) These are "strange children", who would "overthrow the faith of some." (II Tim. 2:18)

Beloved saints of God, let's follow after God's due order! Let's flow with His wonderful theocracy - the only way to keep the unity of the Spirit in the bond of peace. Let's take our place in the government that God has placed upon the shoulders of our wonderful Jesus - the Head of All Things - unto Him be glory in the church forevermore!

Larry Gordon is the Pastor of Cornerstone Faith Center, a dynamic and growing church pioneered by he and his wife Eileen in Sioux City, Iowa. Having traveled and preached in many parts of the world, both Larry and Eileen have a rich understanding of the things of God and impart them consistently to audiences of people whose lives have been enriched and changed victoriously by the truths of the Gospel of Jesus Christ.

For additional copies of

After the Due Order

please write:

Cornerstone Faith Center
6000 Gordon Dr.
Sioux City, IA 51106

or call:

(712) 274-7572